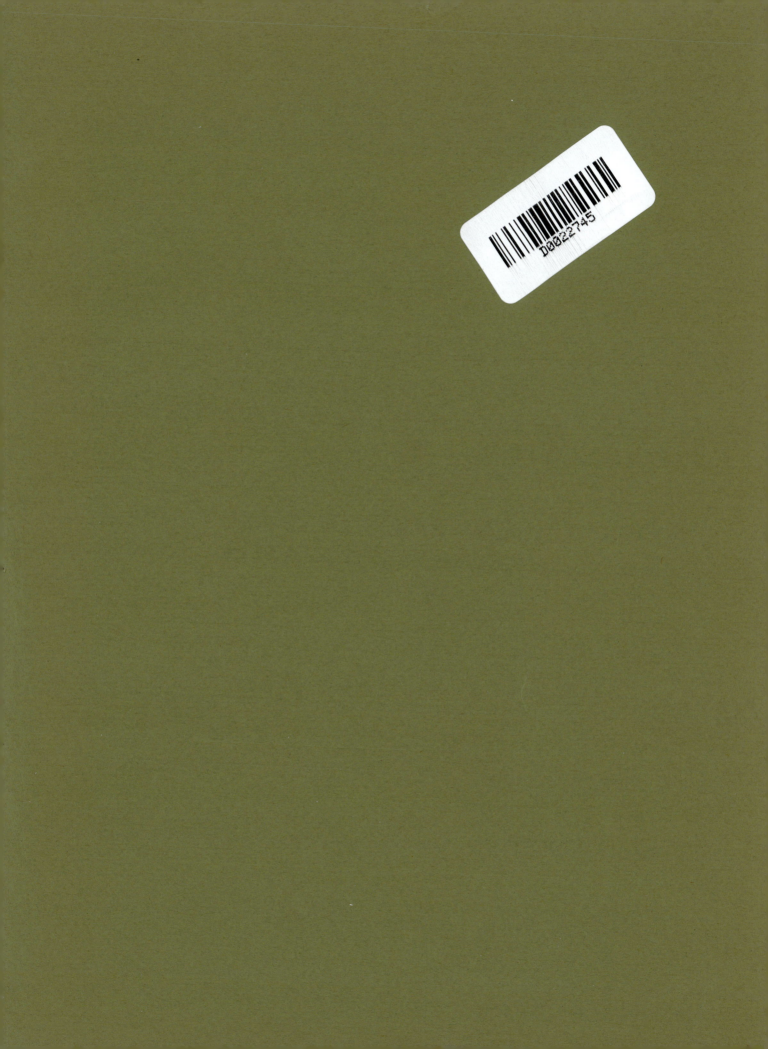

The Art Museum,
Princeton University
January 29–March 26, 1978

Hirshhorn Museum
and Sculpture Garden,
Smithsonian Institution,
Washington, D.C.
April 14–June 26, 1978

Els Quatre Gats

Art in Barcelona around 1900

Marilyn McCully

The Art Museum
Princeton University

Distributed by
Princeton University Press

This project is supported by a grant from the
National Endowment for the Arts in Washington, D.C., a Federal agency.

Jacket/cover/frontispiece: Picasso,
Sebastià Junyer-Vidal and Woman in a Café [33].

Designed by James Wageman.
Composed by The Stinehour Press and
printed by The Meriden Gravure Company.

Photographs were kindly supplied by the museums and collectors
that own the works of art, with the exception of catalogue nos.
1, 2, 11, 14, 15, 18, 21–23, 44, 46, 47, 51–55 (Taylor & Dull);
8 (Uldis Saule); 9, 12, 38, 42 (Mas); 30, 35 (Mas/SPADEM); 27 (Ken Brown);
32 (M. Lynton Gardiner); 45 (Allen Mewbourn); and figs.
1–4, 6, 7, 14, 17 (Mas); 8, 10, 12, 18 (Mas/SPADEM); 19 (Ken Brown).

Library of Congress Catalogue Card Number 77-072143
International Standard Book Number 0-691-03928-3 (clothbound)
International Standard Book Number 0-691-03939-9 (paperbound)

Distributed by Princeton University Press
Princeton, New Jersey 08540
In the United Kingdom
Princeton University Press, Guildford, Surrey

Contents

List of Illustrations

Works Exhibited

Figures

Foreword

The exhibition "Els Quatre Gats" is an important and appropriate one for the Princeton University Art Museum—important because it documents the early development of an artist of the stature of Picasso, and it familiarizes us with the artistic milieu in Barcelona of which he was a part; appropriate because the exhibition derives from the scholarly work and teaching of Marilyn McCully, a member of the faculty of the Department of Art and Archaeology. Many of her students are responsible for entries in the catalogue and were involved, as well, with the installation. We are indebted to Professor McCully for the quality of the exhibition and the catalogue.

The many people who assisted Professor McCully are acknowledged in her preface. I am most appreciative of their cooperation, and I also wish to thank on behalf of the Museum those lenders whose generosity has made this exhibition possible: Rutgers Barclay, Acquavella Galleries; Robert T. Buck, Jr., Director, Albright-Knox Art Gallery; William J. Withrow, Director, and Richard J. Wattenmaker, Chief Curator, Art Gallery of Ontario; Harold Joachim, Curator of Prints and Drawings, Art Institute of Chicago; Audrey Jones Beck, Houston; Sherman E. Lee, Director, and Edward B. Henning, Curator of Modern Art, Cleveland Museum of Art; Frederick J. Cummings, Director, Detroit Institute of Arts; Joan Antoni Maragall, Establecimientos Maragall; Antonio Rocamora, Fundación Manuel Rocamora; Manuel Garí de Arana, Barcelona; Josep Gudiol Ricart, Instituto Amatller; Joseph Rishel, Curator, John G. Johnson Collection; Stephanie Barron, Associate Curator of Modern Art, Los Angeles County Museum of Art; Hermann Bonnin, Museo de Arte Escénico; Juan Barbeta Antonés, Director Técnico, Museo de Arte Moderno; Juan Ainaud de Lasarte, Director, Museos Municipales de Arte de Barcelona; R. Russell Maylone, Curator of Special Collections, Northwestern University Library; and five lenders who wish to remain anonymous.

The complex final stages in the arrangements for loans and shipping of works from Spanish museums were completed with the invaluable assistance of Samuel Dieli, Public Affairs Officer at the American Consulate General's office in Barcelona, and Peter Solomson, Adviser on the Arts, U.S. Department of State, Washington, D.C. Our sincerest thanks are especially due to Maria Teresa Conill, Assistant to the Public Affairs Officer at the American Consulate in Barcelona, whose willingness to help with numerous last-minute details insured our success in obtaining the important Spanish loans. For assistance in arranging loans from the Cau Ferrat in Sitges, we thank the Honorable Josep Tarradellas in Barcelona, and José Llorens, Antoni Mirabent, and Carmen Pascual in Sitges.

For generous support of the exhibition and the catalogue, we are grateful to the National Endowment for the Arts in Washington, D.C., a Federal agency, and to the Publications Fund of the Department of Art and Archaeology, Princeton University.

I wish to thank the staff of the Museum for their work on this exhibition, particularly Allen Rosenbaum, Assistant Director and Curator of Paintings; Virginia Wageman, Director of Publications; and Robert Lafond, Registrar. For their assistance in producing the catalogue under an exacting schedule, we are grateful to James Wageman, who designed it; Freeman Keith of The Stinehour Press; and John F. Peckham of The Meriden Gravure Company.

When the exhibition was first proposed, we were greatly encouraged by the interest of the Hirshhorn Museum and Sculpture Garden, Washington, D.C., where the exhibition will travel following its stay here. Our appreciation and thanks are extended to the staff of the Hirshhorn Museum, especially Abram Lerner, Director; Charles W. Millard, Chief Curator; Cynthia Jaffee McCabe, Curator of Exhibitions; and Howard Fox from the Museum's curatorial staff. We are extremely pleased that this exhibition, which represents so much international cooperation and interest, will be shown in the nation's capital.

Peter C. Bunnell, *Director*
The Art Museum, Princeton University

Preface

The purpose of this exhibition is twofold: to show works by the Spanish artists, many of them relatively unknown in the United States, who met as a group at the café Els Quatre Gats in the years around 1900, and also to consider the work of Picasso's Barcelona period in the context of its time and place. The idea of the exhibition originated when I came to Princeton in 1975. With the encouragement of my colleagues in the Department of Art and Archaeology and in The Art Museum, I began the task of transforming several years of research into an exhibition that would represent the major stylistic concerns of these artists, and characterize the spirit and artistic enthusiasm of their group.

The exhibition was conceived as a small, representative selection, indicative of the wide range of artistic expression fostered by Els Quatre Gats during its relatively short span. The choice of works and artists was difficult, for there were many fascinating individuals whose paths crossed at the café, such as Manolo Hugué, Julio Gonzalez, Joaquín Torres Garcia, Joaquim Mir, and others who are not represented in the exhibition. In order to limit the size of the show yet still convey the character of the period and the group, the following considerations acted as guidelines. First, representative works by the founders of Els Quatre Gats were selected, for among them it was Santiago Rusiñol and Ramón Casas in particular who established the basis of the new painting in Catalonia in the 1890s. The earliest works in the exhibition thus date from 1890. A second generation of artists, such as Ricardo Canals and Isidro Nonell, attracted by the personalities and activities of the founders, enlarged the content and stylistic possibilities of this developing movement. Works by these artists extend the chronological range of the exhibition to 1909. With regard to Picasso, an attempt was made to draw upon North American collections; this search was rewarding because of the quality and broad selection of the works that were found. Finally, the works by other Quatre Gats artists in the show exemplify the variety of creative activity, including poster design, book and magazine illustration, and music, which formed a part of the artistic life of the café and of the period in general.

The catalogue begins with a brief introduction to the concept of *modernismo*, the cultural movement which characterized the period from the mid-1880s until approximately 1910 and which was created in part by the artists who met at Els Quatre Gats. Following is a history of the café from its opening in the summer of 1897 to the last of its advertised activities in 1903. In this history an attempt has been made to describe the nature of the events that were sponsored there and to mention some of the important individuals who contributed to them. These years of intense artistic activity represent a significant chapter in the history of Catalan art generally, and also in the development of the young Picasso. It is hoped that the catalogue will complement the works in the exhibition and help to explain the nature of this special moment in the history of Barcelona and its artists.

The catalogue entries are grouped according to artists, who are presented alphabetically with brief biographies. At the end is a documentary section including music and journals. Whenever possible, the bibliographic and exhibition history of each object is summarized in the entry, with references presented in chronological order. In the case of Picasso, references to the *catalogues raisonnés* by Zervos and Daix are given first in the bibliography section of each entry. In the essays on the objects an attempt has been made to mention stylistic sources for the works of art and to record the documentary value of many of the objects included.

The artist's full name, which according to Spanish custom includes the mother's surname after the father's, is given at the beginning of the biographical section in the catalogue, and in general only the patronymic is used otherwise. To avoid confusion, the artists appear in the list of works exhibited under their fathers' surnames only. An exception is Picasso, who deliberately dropped his father's name Ruíz in about 1900 and adopted his mother's surname as his own.

It should be noted that in order to standardize

the spelling of names and places, a preference has been given to the Catalan unless the Castilian version was originally used extensively. The current tendency to use Catalan versions of all names (such as Isidre Nonell or Ricard Opisso) accounts for the variation found in contemporary publications.

In the fall of 1976 I gave a graduate seminar at Princeton on the topic "Barcelona 1900." The students in that seminar contributed several of the catalogue entries, which are initialed by the individual authors: Eric Apfelstadt, Nina M. Athanassoglou, Perry Chapman, Marc Freidus, Diana Hulick, Amy McClellan, and Robert McVaugh. Two Princeton undergraduates, Xavier Richardson and Deborah Clarke, also provided research assistance.

In the preparation of the exhibition and the catalogue I have received valuable help from many people, and welcome this opportunity to acknowledge their contribution to the project. To the museums and collectors who generously agreed to lend works to the exhibition, and who have allowed us to reproduce them in the catalogue, I express my gratitude for their cooperation. I wish to thank Mr. Juan Ainaud de Lasarte, Director, Museos de Arte de Barcelona, Mr. Juan Barbeta, Director Técnico de los Museos de Arte de Barcelona, Ms. Cristina Mendoza, and Ms. Cecilia Vidal for their special efforts on my behalf in Barcelona.

At The Art Museum at Princeton, I received most welcome guidance and assistance from Peter C. Bunnell, Director, and Allen Rosenbaum, Assistant Director. Virginia Wageman, the Museum's director of publications, and Robert Lafond, the registrar, generously gave of their time and handled the many complicated details of the preparation of both the show and the catalogue. I am especially grateful to Mary Laing for her expert editing of the manuscript and thoughtful contributions to the text. In addition, Kathy Dobbins and Lynda Gillman deserve special thanks for their careful and attentive typing of the manuscript. At the Hirshhorn Museum I am grateful to Mr. Charles W. Millard, Chief Curator, and Ms. Cynthia McCabe, Curator of Exhibitions, for their cooperation.

Funds for exhibition research and travel were made possible by grants from the Department of Art and Archaeology and the University Committee on Research in the Humanities and Social Sciences at Princeton. The cost of the exhibition and catalogue was generously supported by a grant from the National Endowment for the Arts.

Many people have helped me during the past years on my research concerning Catalan art, and I would like to acknowledge here their generosity and interest in my work. I am especially grateful to Mr. Joan Antoni Maragall and the staff of the Sala Parés, and Mr. Josep Gudiol of the Instituto Amatller for their continued support and help. In addition, special thanks are due to Ms. Elisenda Sala for her untiring assistance in the collection of some of these materials, and to Professor José Miguel Sobré for his corrections of my translations. Finally, I wish to thank Thomas A. Wills for his advice at every stage of the project and his confidence in my work.

Els
Quatre
Gats

Modernismo in Catalonia

The period between 1890 and 1910 in Catalonia was characterized by a spirit of cultural and political optimism, and a renewal of interest in a regional art movement. This cultural *renaixensa* (renascence) held that Catalonia, with its own language and history, was a separate entity that was closer in its attitudes to the rest of Europe than it was to Spain, within whose geographical limits it was bound. The cultivation of an art movement, known as *modernismo*, was essentially part of this larger cultural development in the history of the Catalans.

The term *modernismo* as used here refers to the cultural manifestations, including painting, that were initiated in Catalonia in the 1890s by the founders of Els Quatre Gats and the group that surrounded them. These activities included the popular *modernista* festivals held in the nearby seaside village of Sitges, which were sponsored by Rusiñol with the help of Utrillo, Romeu, and Pichot among others. The festivals included art exhibitions, opera and theater productions, such as a Catalan translation of Maeterlinck's *L'Intruse*, dance and literary sessions, and special tributes to artists such as El Greco. The frequent exhibition of paintings by Casas, Rusiñol, and their friends in the 1890s in Barcelona led also to a stylistic definition of *modernismo* which referred to this body of work.

In recent years the term *modernismo* has acquired a somewhat different connotation referring principally to architecture and the decorative arts—for example, furniture, jewelry, bookbindings, and a variety of everyday objects. In that sense, the term comes closer to describing the later, international art-nouveau movement rather than the specifically Catalan art movement. A further distinction must also be made with reference to *modernista* literature. In an excellent article defining *modernismo*, Joan Lluis Marfany notes that the term was applied as early as 1884 to the literature, science, and art of the Catalan intellectual movement.[1] At the same time, however, it was used in Madrid to describe the Castilian literary movement, which is quite distinct from Catalan activities, although mutual curiosity between the two existed. Indeed, a large literature developed in Catalonia during this period, and influential figures such as Rusiñol were important contributors. In order to limit the focus of this discussion to painting and the specific activities of the café Els Quatre Gats, literary *modernismo* will be mentioned only incidentally, and architecture and the decorative arts will be considered only where they contribute to a clarification of the art that grew up around the Quatre Gats group.[2]

In general the term *modernismo*, when used to describe painting, refers to the work produced by Santiago Rusiñol and Ramón Casas, in addition to the artists who gathered around them, during the period beginning in Paris in approximately 1890 to the closing of Els Quatre Gats in 1903. Although most of these artists continued painting after that date, the dispersal of the Quatre Gats group marks the moment when they began to work separately; in so doing, they pursued highly personal styles. A definition of *modernista* painting becomes complicated not only by the mixed use of the term already mentioned, but also by the variety of subjects and styles that these painters developed. A consideration of its earliest appearance in the work of Rusiñol and Casas is fundamental to understanding this development.

Modernista painting began to emerge as an identifiable trend, both in subject matter and in theory, in the early 1890s. By this date Rusiñol and Casas had assumed the leadership of a "new school" of painting, which was decidedly affected by their contact with French art.[3] Most of the work that won

---

1 Marfany, "Sobre el significat del terme 'modernisme.'"

2 Considerable attention has been paid to architecture and the decorative arts in publications concerning *modernismo*; see especially Ráfols, *Modernismo y modernistas*; Cirici, *El arte modernista catalán*; and, more recently, Cervera, *Modernismo*. A forthcoming contribution is Judith Rohrer's doctoral dissertation at Columbia University, "La Nova Escola Catalana: Architectural Politics in Barcelona, 1880–1910."

3 Rusiñol and Casas began to exhibit on an annual basis in Barcelona at the Sala Parés in 1890. The new tendency in Catalan painting that was detected in their work was first called the *nova*

them this recognition was produced in Paris, where they spent several months each year in their apartment over the famed dance hall, the Moulin de la Galette.[4] There in the heart of Montmartre they lived a life that was constantly in touch with the artistic currents of the *fin de siècle*. Their friendships in the world of the arts ranged from cabaret regulars, such as Toulouse-Lautrec, Aristide Bruant, Yvette Guilbert, and Erik Satie, to artists such as Puvis de Chavannes and Carrière. During those years Rusiñol and Casas regularly participated in the prestigious Champ de Mars Salon, and in 1891 they also exhibited at the Salon des Indépendants in the company of the neo-impressionists and the young Nabi brotherhood. The blend of influences that they drew from this French experience, combined with their own Spanish background, formed the basis for a new school of painting, which developed and flourished as *modernismo* in the 1890s in Catalonia.

The two fundamental components of *modernista* painting as developed by Rusiñol and Casas are the concepts of naturalism and "symbolist" suggestion. A theoretical approach based upon these concepts allowed the Catalans to enlarge their range of subject matter and to experiment with techniques which, while certainly not revolutionary compared to the French art which inspired them, constituted a major step forward in the formulation of a new art movement in Catalonia.

For Rusiñol, naturalism meant the truthful recording of nature by the artist.[5] Subjects selected from nature contrasted with the ideal world created in the painter's studio and signified his acceptance of the real world as worthy of his attention. This attitude had the effect of extending the range of subject matter covered by Rusiñol's concept of naturalism to everyday life. His works of the early 1890s included both landscapes and scenes drawn from his own Parisian experience, and in this sense they were literally modernist. In a review of Rusiñol's 1890 show in Barcelona, Miguel Utrillo called attention to the power of the simple images of "interiors deprived of all refinements, floors worn out by a hundred generations of boors, fields sterile from too many harvests" and "finally the desolation of misery, the nudity of poverty, the dense cape of mildew which covers the sordidness of miserable things."[6] In an attempt to capture the effects of atmosphere and light, Rusiñol adjusted his palette according to the setting and the time of day; the ashen tonality, "the dense cape of mildew," which was used by both Rusiñol and Casas during this period to depict misty gardens and darkened interiors, thus became a means of evoking mood. Rusiñol felt that in accurately recording nature, the artist could re-create the emotional quality of the subject he had chosen.

Ramón Casas, who shared an equally influential position among younger Spanish artists, was less of a romantic than Rusiñol, and in France saw the potential for new subject matter and painterly techniques. He quickly began to paint scenes from contemporary life, particularly fashionable women and places of entertainment such as the dance hall and café. Casas's approach was also based upon naturalism and, particularly in his intimate interiors, he succeeded in conveying mood through painterly expression. In questions of technique, he experimented to a greater extent than Rusiñol with a loosened brush stroke and color, qualities which are still called "impressionist" in Spain, and his use of flattened

escola (new school) by critics such as Antonio Garcia Llansó in "Pintura y escultura," *La Ilustración* (19 Oct. 1890), 41.

4 Rusiñol and Casas collaborated on a series of articles for *La Vanguardia* describing their experiences in Paris. These articles were published as a book, *Desde el molino*, in 1894 by the Barcelona publishing house L'Avenç. For a more detailed discussion of this period, see McCully, "Els Quatre Gats," 1975, 16–55.

5 A tradition of naturalism was well established in both French art and literature, and Rusiñol's understanding of the concept comes from that tradition. In addition, the Catalan landscape painters, the so-called School of Olot, contributed to Rusiñol's earliest interest in the Barbizon painters; for further discussion, see McCully, "Els Quatre Gats," 1975, 3–10.

In 1891 Casellas attempted to formulate a definition of *modernista* painting in his *credo*, which is based upon the concept of naturalism and Rusiñol's work in particular. According to Jordà

(*Ramón Casas, pintor*, 38), Casellas's *credo* was read aloud among young artists as a manifesto of the new school of Catalan art.

6 Miguel Utrillo, "Los pintores españoles en el salón de Paris," *La Vanguardia* (7 July 1890), Archivo Rusiñol, vol. 1, 43–44.

shapes and shallow space was certainly inspired by the growing sense of decoration among artists such as Toulouse-Lautrec and some of the Nabis. By the late 1890s Casas was able to translate these artistic concerns into creative poster and illustration design, which in turn influenced this popular aspect of the *modernista* movement.

By the mid-1890s Rusiñol and Casas began to direct more of their efforts towards the encourage-ment of the Catalan cultural movement, of which their painting was now an integral part. As a result of their trips to Paris, they brought with them a rich exposure to the artistic and literary trends of the late nineteenth century outside of Spain, and proceeded with enthusiasm to communicate new ideas and stimulate a generation of young artists, first at the *modernista* festivals in Sitges and then at the turn of the century at Els Quatre Gats.

Els Quatre Gats, Its Artists and Activities

The Opening, 1897

Els Quatre Gats, advertised as a *cerveseria-taverna-hostal* ("beer hall-tavern-inn"), opened its doors to the public on 12 June 1897, in the recently constructed Casa Martí, designed by Puig i Cadafalch.[1] The building, which was the architect's first important commission, incorporated current taste for the medieval and a rich variety of local Catalan crafts. In 1897 Bonaventura Bassegoda called it a "free translation" of late Catalan gothic and an homage to contemporary Catalonia.[2]

The building (fig. 1), which still stands today, faces Calle Montesión, no. 3-bis, and was called by Casellas in 1902, a "mixture of archaeology and *modernismo* . . . of love for the old and a passion for the new . . . symbolized in that very special building by Puig i Cadafalch."[3] The entrance is characterized by two oversized gothic arches, which are repeated along the side of the building, located on Pasaje de San José.[4] Above the main entrance there was a metal sign in the shape of two arched cats, black on one side and gray on the other [35], representing the name of the tavern, "The Four Cats."

"Four cats" is a colloquial Catalan expression for "only a few people" and the name of Els Quatre Gats is derived from this.[5] It had another, more specific source, which can be traced to the Parisian experience of the four principal animators of the establishment: Pere Romeu, Santiago Rusiñol, Ramón Casas, and Miguel Utrillo. Each of the originators, who can themselves be considered "the four cats," shared an interest in the celebrated Parisian café Le Chat Noir, "The Black Cat," whose creator, Rodolphe Salis, had recently died. Their recollections were to form the

essential basis for the activities of its Barcelona counterpart. At the same time, this café-tavern also drew on the native Spanish tradition of the *tertulia*, a regular social gathering for talk and the exchange of ideas.

The main room of El Quatre Gats or *sala gran* (fig. 2), filled with popular ceramic art and other collected odds and ends, was the center of entertainment, site of exhibitions and refreshments. Its usual focal point and the place for animated discussion was one of the tables designed by Puig i Cadafalch. From the beginning the artists who met there covered the walls of the various rooms with their drawings and paintings. The largest was a depiction of Romeu and Casas riding a tandem bicycle [10], painted for the café by Casas in 1897.

At the rear of a small stage used for puppet theater, a decorative, ceramic frame contained a curious *modernista* painting (fig. 3) with the saying *L'home que be vulga viure, Bons aliments y molt riure* ("The man who lives a good, simple life, [needs] good food and much laughter"). In the central portion, a woman, as though asleep, drifts through a field of irises. In the sky, floating towards her, as if to invade her dreams, are various figures in caricature, including a skeleton, a Spanish *guardia civil*, the devil, and a few portraits. One of these can be identified as the proprietor, Pere Romeu, wearing a nightgown (suggesting that it may be *his* dream). The unexplained allegory was probably designed by Utrillo and Casas, who collaborated on publicity for Els Quatre Gats. Below this section, the emblem designed by Casas for the café was re-created in ceramic tiles. The same design, Romeu's head next to four cats, was also to appear on ceramic beer mugs and on various printed invitations and handouts.

Rusiñol wrote two announcements that served as public invitations. They bore a gothic-styled letterhead designed by his friend from Sitges, Miró, in which an arched cat stands proudly on a shield bearing the Roman numeral IV and three other cats sur-

1 This account is based upon chapter 4 of my dissertation; see McCully, "Els Quatre Gats," 1975, 179–234.

2 Bonaventura Bassegoda, "Notas artísticas," *La Renaixensa* (27 July 1897), 1129–32.

3 Casellas, "Puig i Cadafalch," 81.

4 Pasaje de San José was then called Pasaje de la Patriarca.

5 For an anecdotal account of the naming of the café, see Saltiró, "*Quatre Gats*" o una tertulia de alegres bohemios, 5.

1 Exterior view of Casa Martí in Barcelona, ca. 1899

round the striped Catalan flag. In the more widely circulated announcement, the attractions of the neo-gothic building and its museum-like contents are combined with allusions to *fin-de-siècle* decadence:

> This stopping place is an inn for the disillusioned; it is a corner full of warmth for those who long for home; it is a museum for those who look for illuminations for the soul; it is a tavern and stopping place for those who love the shadow of butterflies, and the essence of a cluster of grapes; it is a gothic beer hall for lovers of the North and an Andalusian patio for lovers of the South; it is a place to cure the ills of our century, and a place for friendship

and harmony for those who enter bowing beneath the portals of the house.[6]

Unlike the Chat Noir and its intimate, select atmosphere, the Quatre Gats group made a concerted effort to attract a wider public. The reason was their underlying hope to contribute in some way to the glory of Catalonia and this moment of cultural renewal and optimism.

One month after the inauguration of Els Quatre Gats, the first of many exhibitions to be held in the

6 For the full text, see McCully, "Els Quatre Gats," 1975, appendix XVI.

sala gran was opened. It included works by Bonnin, Canals, Casas, Espert, Mir, Nonell, Pichot, Rusiñol, Torent, and Utrillo. The catalogue, which bears the standard emblem designed by Casas, announced a "Breu relació dels dibuixos i estudis al oli fi que alguns pintors han exposat a la sala dels quatre Gats. Els Demés Parroquians podrian veure-la i dir-hi lo que 'ls sembli, del Diumenge 11 al Diumenge 18" ("Small gathering of drawings and oil studies which several local painters have exhibited in the main room of the Quatre Gats. Other neighbors can see them, and say what they think, from Sunday the 11th to Sunday the 18th").

La Vanguardia reviewed the show, as did several other local papers, and the general opinion was that the intimate surroundings of Els Quatre Gats were quite appropriate for small exhibitions of *modernista* content. The *La Vanguardia* reviewer thought that

the new exhibition space promised to be an extremely interesting *salonnet* or *petite chapelle* of the type best exemplified by similar establishments on the streets of Le Pelletier (Le Barc de Boutteville) and Lafitte (Vollard) in Paris.

Recollections of Paris were strong among the works exhibited by the leaders of *modernismo*. Casas, who was praised for his great versatility, showed paintings such as *Record del Molí* (*Memory of the Moulin de la Galette*). Rusiñol, who exhibited *Erik Satie quan era de la Rose + Croix*, honored his friend, the contemporary composer, with this "true effigy of Erik Satie playing his *Sonneries* on the piano."[7] Utrillo showed his *Portrait of Suzanne Valadon* [49], as well as decorative drawings that reflected his interest in French lithography and Japanese prints.

7 "Exposición de 'Els Quatre Gats,'" *La Vanguardia* (16 July 1897), 4.

Sombras artísticas

One of the most popular attractions initiated in late 1897 was the shadow puppet theater, *sombras artísticas*, which was originated and directed by Utrillo, with the assistance of Romeu, who was also experienced in its production.[8] Their model was a similar feature at Le Chat Noir in Paris, the *ombres japonaises*, which had been introduced there by Henri Rivière. Early productions were based simply upon the principle of moving cut-out shapes in front of an illuminated screen to produce shadows, while songs and recitations accompanied the performance. The addition of colored glass, electricity, and movement in the figures themselves introduced new possibilities for originality in the production of these curious plays in

the 1890s. In an article for *La Vanguardia*, Rusiñol specifically mentioned Utrillo's engineering innovations at his own shadow puppet theater at the Auberge du Clou in 1891. He wrote that Utrillo "knows how to bring together art and science as brothers, to obtain rare contrasts of color with changing effects of light."[9] The idea of setting up the *sombras artísticas* at Els Quatre Gats was thus due to its established popularity in Paris and also to the creative aspect that Utrillo believed would appeal to members of the group.

The opening of the *sombras artísticas* was held at Els Quatre Gats on 29 December 1897, and Utrillo gave an inaugural speech explaining the history of the theater entitled "La sombra arqueológica, l'elephant." The program began with a poem by the popular Catalan poet, Joan Maragall, entitled *Montserrat*, which was accompanied by music composed by Morera and sets designed by Utrillo. Next was a

8 Romeu had studied the shadow puppet theater at Le Chat Noir and joined Léon-Charles Mârot's group, which took the attraction to the Chicago World's Fair in 1893. In addition to Romeu, the participants in Mârot's Les Ombres Parisiennes included Utrillo, another Catalan Federic Homdedeu, Henry Somm, Steinlen, Théodore Savagner, Samp, and the Chat Noir pianist, Charles de Sivry. Listed on the program were shadow puppet plays created by Somm, Steinlen, and Utrillo; for further discussion, see McCully, "Els Quatre Gats," 1975, 42–45.

9 Rusiñol, "El reino de las sombras," *La Vanguardia* (31 March 1892); see also Rusiñol, *Obres completes*, 1914–15.

4 Ramón Casas and Miguel Utrillo.
Poster: *Sombras: Quatre Gats*,
lithograph, 1897.
Private collection

poem by the art critic Jordà, entitled *Nadala*, accompanied by music by Joan Gay and drawings by Pichot. At the end came the work *El viaje humorístico Quatre Gats y un vestit negre o en Pere Romeu pel mon* ("The humorous Quatre Gats trip and a black outfit or Pere Romeu around the world"), with words by Enric de Fuentes and drawings by Casas.

The first presentation was reported in the press and described as having "the character of a small intellectual party," because of the distinguished audience.[10] The feature was deliberately aimed at adults and achieved its success through the fruitful collaboration of the various artists, musicians, and writers involved.

With the exception of special children's features on 6 January and 2 February (which were held in the afternoon as opposed to the normal late evening sessions), the inaugural program ran until mid-February, when a second series was initiated. The new program offered *Nit de lluna*, with words and drawings by Juli Vallmitjana, and a biblical poem in two acts, *Jesus de Nazareth*, accompanied by fourteen drawings by Lluis Bonnin and music by Francesc Ginesta. This program lasted until the first part of

April, when the *sombras* were discontinued because of Holy Week. After that date no new programs were advertised.

The first poster executed for Els Quatre Gats appeared in connection with the *sombras* and was designed by Ramón Casas and Miguel Utrillo (fig. 4). Printed by the lithographers A. Utrillo y Rialp, the appearance of this *cartel* quickly reached the attention of Barcelona critics, one of whom called it "perhaps one of the best that has appeared from the Barcelona printing press . . . [this poster] will undoubtedly be the object of pursuit among *aficionados* and collectors."[11] Casas was responsible for the compositional placement of the figures and lettering; Utrillo added the superimposed decorative effects, notably the cloak of the woman at the left. At the rear of the scene is a group of café personalities— Casas, Utrillo, Rusiñol, Zuloaga, and Meifren—to the left of the shadow puppet screen, with Romeu to the right. Copies of this poster can be seen hanging on the walls of the interior (fig. 3), to the upper left and right of the *modernista* allegory.

10 "Espectáculos," *La Publicidad* (30 Dec. 1897), 2.

11 *La Publicidad* (21 Dec. 1897), 2.

The Exhibitions of 1898

In November 1898 the first of a series of one-man shows opened in the *sala gran* of Els Quatre Gats. It featured the Asturian artist Dario de Regoyos (1857–1913). The works included in this exhibition were the illustrations for the book *España negra*, a collaborative effort between Regoyos and the Belgian writer Emile Verhaeren. Utrillo wrote an important biographical sketch and review of the show in the magazine *Luz*, no. 8, 1898, and several of Regoyos's drawings were reproduced in issues 8–12. Regoyos's presence in Barcelona was welcomed, for his earlier experiences in Brussels as a member of Les Vingt and his travels in England, Germany, and France, where he knew many artists personally, were discussed among the group which gathered at the Quatre Gats *tertulia*.

The next show, immediately following Regoyos's exhibit, featured drawings by Isidro Nonell. It ran from December 4 to 20 in the *sala gran* and was advertised by an invitation, *Exposició de dibuixos de Nonell Monturiol*, which depicted an old woman seated on a bench.[12] The exhibition included Nonell's famous series *Cretins de Bohí*, based on the strange group of people he had discovered in the isolated village of Bohí in the Pyrenees, and it complemented the theme of *España negra* which had preceded his show. Critics linked Nonell's name with artists such as Goya, Gavarni, Forain, and Rops, because of his inclination to depict the injustices and ills of society. Nonell's interests, however, lay less in social commentary than in the straightforward sketching and observation of life around him, and in experimentation with techniques. According to a reviewer, the strange effects of some of his *dibujos fritos* (drawings on paper subsequently dipped in paint varnish) created the illusion of precious fragments from the past, "as if we had passed before them in some museum of *trecento* works, gilded and blackened with age, but still retaining original areas of color." The same reviewer continued the comparison by observing that "like the works [of the primitives] Nonell's drawings also have an absence of convention in drawing and pose that in substance comes nearer to our own epoch."[13] The significance of this show at Els Quatre Gats, and of Nonell's contribution to *modernista* painting in general, was to generate interest in the subject of the poor and unfortunate, as well as to introduce new stylistic possibilities, such as the formal simplifications of his drawing style.

Exhibitions at Els Quatre Gats also followed an informal schedule and there are undated references to shows by Ricardo Canals, Ignacio Zuloaga, Luisa Vidal, and the Benlliure brothers.

12 Jardí, *Nonell*, no. 42.

13 F. C., "Exposición Nonell en los Quatre Gats," *La Publicidad* (6 Dec. 1898), 2.

Putxinel-lis

A second puppet theater, *putxinel-lis* (*puchinel-lis*), was added as an attraction in late 1898. This new feature, primarily aimed towards a youthful audience, was publicized by the striking *Puchinel-lis* poster by Casas [12]. One of the most memorable descriptions of the theater comes from the pen of the writer and friend of Rusiñol, Rubén Darío, who visited Els Quatre Gats in late 1898:

It was the day of marionettes and [Romeu] invited me to see the feature. Els Quatre Gats is something like a copy of Le Chat Noir of Paris with Pere Romeu for Salis, a silent Salis, a gentleman *cabaretier* who I believe is a painter of a certain substance. . . . He himself led me to the little room of the show where more than one hundred persons would not fit. [It was] decorated with posters, pen and ink drawings, sepias, impressions, sketches, and also finished paintings by the young and new Barcelona painters. Standing out among them were those which bore the signature of the master Rusiñol. The puppets are something like those which in their time attracted the curiosity of Paris with the mysteries of Bouchor, little pieces by Richepin, and others. For similar actors of wood, Maeterlinck composed his most beautiful dramas of profundity and dreams. There in the Quatre Gats they are pretty well handled. . . . The bocks [of beer] circulated to the high-pitched voices of the puppets. Naturally, the puppets of Quatre Gats speak in Catalan and I could hardly understand what they were talking about in the scene. . . . The decorations are true little paintings, and one sees that those who have organized the diminutive theater have done so with love and care.[14]

The *putxinel-lis* theater was performed on the little platform beneath the tiled legend, *L'home que be vulga viure, Bons aliments y molt riure* (fig. 3); in

14 Darío, *España contemporánea*, 16–17.

fact, the *modernista* allegory which appears in the photograph may be one of the sets Darío admired.[15] In addition to Julio Pi, the regular puppeteer, others at Els Quatre Gats participated in the promotion and production of the *putxinel-lis*. The young sculptor, Manolo Hugué, who was introduced to the tavern by Pichot, rapidly became an avid fan of Pi and his magical theater; he studied the puppets' grace of movement in Pi's hands and aided in productions. In addition to Pi's own repertory, there were contributions of plays created by the Quatre Gats group. In May 1899 a competition was announced in the magazine *Quatre Gats* for an original drama on a "feline" theme appropriate for presentation at the marionette theater. For prizes Ramón Casas offered an original drawing for the best one-act comedy, Juli Vallmitjana an enamel work for drama, and Manolo a sculpted bust for the best work of magic. The popularity of the *putxinel-lis* insured its place as a regular feature at Els Quatre Gats until the café closed several years later.

15 Another amusing traveler's description of activities in the tavern is recorded by Thirlmere, *Letters from Catalonia*, 366–72.

Posters

At Els Quatre Gats, as we have seen, posters were created specifically for the café, such as *Sombras: Quatre Gats* (fig. 4) by Casas and Utrillo, Casas's *Puchinel-lis: 4 Gats* [12], and in 1900, his *4 Gats: Pere Romeu* [13]. In addition, both Catalan and foreign posters decorated the interior and special poster events, including exhibitions and competitions, were occasionally held there (see chronology). When Rubén Darío visited the café in early 1899, he described the streets of Barcelona as a "springtime of posters or *affiches* which delight the eyes in their festival of lines and color," and he attributed the great popularity of the medium to the Quatre Gats group.[16] Rusiñol, Casas, Utrillo, and other members of the group had,

16 Darío, *España contemporánea*, 15.

in fact, contributed to the general interest in posters that developed in the late 1890s as part of the Catalan cultural movement.

Posters and graphic design in general quickly became associated with *modernista* activities, and for this reason the stylistic connotation of *modernismo* was expanded. The appearance of certain motifs, such as stylized flowers and lettering characterized by serpentine line, reflected the awareness of the more international decorative movement of this period, art nouveau. The accessibility of printed images and the exhibition of foreign posters in Barcelona provided Catalan artists with a ready source of first-hand examples of new graphic design from all over Europe and the United States. The promotion of this aspect of the art movement was due in part to the efforts of the Quatre Gats group, both at the café and in journals, and to individuals such as J. B. Parés at his gallery, the Sala Parés.

The first major show of foreign posters in Barcelona had been organized by J. B. Parés in 1896. Represented were book and magazine covers, including a special display of *Jugend*, the German illustrated journal, and graphic works by Besnard, Puvis de Chavannes, Chéret, Dudley Hardy, Grasset, Bradley, Hansall, Forain, Steinlen, Toulouse-Lautrec, Toroop, Mucha, and several others.[17]

In 1897 Adrià Gual won recognition at the first officially sanctioned poster competition among Catalan artists held at the Palacio de Bellas Artes in Barcelona. During the summer of 1899 Utrillo and

Casas, as editors of *Pèl & Ploma*, in collaboration with their friend the artist Alexandre de Riquer, sponsored a poster exhibition at the Barcelona Ateneo featuring the work of Catalan artists. In an editorial in *Pèl & Ploma* (1 July 1899) concerning the exhibition, a clear indication is given of the importance attached to the poster. As an easily duplicated artistic product, it was considered a means of communicating the developing Catalan art movement to audiences outside Spain. By the end of 1899 international recognition had indeed been achieved, for posters by Catalan artists, such as Casas's *Anis del Mono* [11], were being collected in both Paris and London, and reproductions of representative work were appearing in foreign journals.[18]

17 J. C. y R., "Sala Parés," *La Veu de Catalunya*, no. 47 (22 Nov. 1896), 557.

18 See, for example, Pylax, "New Posters"; and Deschamps, "L'Affiche espagnole."

The Exhibitions of 1899

The first individual show at Els Quatre Gats in 1899 was held in February and featured Ramón Pichot. The selection of works in the show, including both drawings and paintings, was destined for exhibition later that year in Paris, Berlin, and Madrid in the hope that Pichot's work would be recognized outside Catalonia. Raimon Casellas, who had begun writing the art column for the new daily *La Veu de Catalunya* (previously a weekly), reviewed the show and credited Pichot with great advances over previous exhibitions.[19] His subject matter was described as both "fantastic" and "gloomy," reflecting the symbolist imagery of his illustrations for Rusiñol's book *Fulls de la vida* [36] of the previous year. In addition, there were scenes of Spanish customs and one oil painting that Casellas considered to be the most important work in the show, *Espanya vella*. In this interior scene, Pichot was able to produce the effect of an apparition through his special use of light; this lumi-

nous quality became a characteristic of his work in general, as in *Boulevard at Sunset* [37].

On 25 April 1899 a new show was inaugurated, featuring a young artist from Lerida, Xavier Gosé (1876–1915). Some forty drawings, most of which were colored, were exhibited. They were described by Casellas as "influenced by that sadness, that oppression which the draftsmen of our days seem to enjoy in the interpretation of human life."[20] Although Gosé, like Nonell and Pichot, chose gloomy themes, Casellas noted in *La Veu de Catalunya* that a certain intimacy, coziness, and elegance could be detected in Gosé's work, which distinguished it from that of his companions.

During the period Gosé frequented Els Quatre Gats, he worked on several illustrated publications, including the magazine *Quatre Gats*, for which his drawings served as covers for no. 6 and no. 9. In about 1900 he moved to Paris and there worked as an

19 Raimon Casellas, "Exposició Pitxot," *La Veu de Catalunya* (23 Feb. 1899).

20 Raimon Casellas, "Exposició Gosé, IV Gats," *La Veu de Catalunya* (25 April 1899).

5 Xavier Gosé. Magazine cover:
Flamenco Dancers, for *Cocorico*,
1–15 October 1900

illustrator for many French periodicals, such as *Cocorico* and *Le Rire*. Gosé's cover for *Cocorico* of 1–15 October 1900, for example, shows a use of line that enlivens both the dancing figure and the composition as a whole (fig. 5). The elegance Casellas detected in Gosé's Quatre Gats drawings had developed into a fluid linear technique, which complemented the subjects of fashionable women and scenes of entertainment that characterized his illustrations of these years.

In May 1899, Evelí Torent—whose portrait by his friend Picasso dates from that year [25]—opened an exhibition of drawings and paintings in the *sala gran*. It was described by the new *La Vanguardia* art critic, Alfredo Opisso, as "one of the most interesting that

has been celebrated [at Els Quatre Gats]."[21] Opisso continued by pointing out that Torent exemplified the new tendencies in Catalan art and that the Quatre Gats exhibitions were beginning to have an influence on public taste. According to Opisso, the distinguishing factor in the new style, which implies Rusiñol's contribution to *modernista* painting, was the untiring insistence on recording nature, not as something "invariable and fixed," but rather "in its constant instability."

The next exhibition at the tavern was anticipated by what was described as "an extremely elegant poster and lovely invitation" drawn by the featured

21 Alfredo Opisso, "Exposición Torent," *La Vanguardia* (20 May 1899).

artist, Josep Dalmau (1867–1937). The show included drawings, both pastel and pencil, and several oils which were noted for the influence of Velázquez and contemporary artists such as Rusiñol.

The real importance of Dalmau's contact with Els Quatre Gats came several years later. The avant-garde milieu of the Barcelona café had caused Dalmau to consider seriously his own role in the promotion of modern art in Catalonia. His activities as a collector and gallery owner in Barcelona in later years led to his support of new Catalan artists, such as Joan Miró and Salvador Dalí. In addition, his gallery was the principal location of Catalan Dada and included the presence of Picabia and his *391*, which was published there in 1917.

Illustrated Journals

The increasing popularity of illustrated art journals in the 1890s led to the founding in 1899 of a magazine at Els Quatre Gats called *Quatre Gats*. Its inspiration can be traced once again to Le Chat Noir, which had originated an artistic journal by the same name as the cabaret more than a decade before.

The first issue of *Quatre Gats*, in the Catalan language, appeared during the second week of February and fourteen other numbers followed. In an opening article, "A tothom" by Pere Romeu, readers were welcomed to a weekly publication that was intended to be purely artistic and literary, without political overtones, except for its role in promoting the splendor of *la terra catalana*. The publication was also a voice for the café, and features such as *putxinel·lis* programs, exhibitions, and special events were mentioned regularly. Included in the first issue were the prize-winning poems and compositions from a literary competition sponsored by Els Quatre Gats. The titles reflected the theme of this promotional event and poems included "A una gata," by Conrat Roure, "El gat dels frarers," by J. Serra y Constanzo, and the first-prize winner, "La abada dels gats," by Guillem A. Tell y Lafont. Finally, there was the winning iconographic history of the *bestia nacional*, entitled "Lo gat," by Joan Bta. Martí y Navarre. Later issues also included poems from this same competition, as well as new works solicited from café regulars.

Pere Romeu's column, "Sobre la taula," recounted weekly events and local gossip from the café *tertulia*.

The outside activities of the Quatre Gats group were also mentioned and included participation in artistic events in Madrid or Paris and in local competitions. Publications by members of the group, such as Rusiñol's *Fulls de la vida* [36], were always announced, and the personal activities of Rusiñol and Casas were followed quite closely, including all their travels to Paris or Sitges. Individual exhibitions at the café were noticed and illustrations of exhibited works were often reproduced in the magazine.

Covers for the different issues, printed in one or two colors, were contributed by Casas, Mir, Pichot, Nonell, Rusiñol, Gosé, Vázquez, Opisso, Riquer, Garcia-Escarre, Torent, and Mulder. Each issue contained several illustrations accompanying the variety of articles and poems that filled the four-page publication. Advertisements, including publicity for Els Quatre Gats, were printed at the end of the issue.

The last issue of *Quatre Gats* appeared on 25 May 1899 with the statement that a new and more sophisticated publication by the name of *Pèl & Ploma* would replace it. An announcement of the new magazine appeared on 3 June 1899 in *La Vanguardia*, noting that "it is a publication of the stature of the most celebrated foreign journals in the genre cultivated by Forain, Steinlen and others and constitutes an artistic, refined note . . . which should awaken and animate [its readers]."[22]

Pèl & Ploma [52] was longer lived than any of its

22 *La Vanguardia* (3 June 1899), 2.

immediate predecessors, lasting from 1899 to 1903, and the events and personalities recorded in it during those years make it the most significant journal to emerge from the *modernista* art world. As for *Quatre Gats*, Utrillo served as literary editor and Casas, who shared in the financing of the venture, was art editor. Headquarters for the publication were located at Casas's Barcelona studio on Paseo de Gracia, no. 96.

During the first two years of publication, *Pèl & Ploma* followed a regular format of four pages with a one- or two-color cover for each weekly issue. The cover was most often a Casas drawing and various artists contributed illustrations for the feature article; occasional posters and paintings were also reproduced. The magazine was published in Catalan, although there was a brief attempt in 1900 to issue an edition in Castilian for the purpose of reaching a wider audience in the Americas and the rest of Spain. Announcements of exhibitions, new publications, and advertisements were included at the end of the journal.

The lead article of the first issue was devoted to Rusiñol and his latest play, *L'alegria que passa* [43], about a troupe of traveling entertainers. Several drawings by Casas and Rusiñol illustrated Utrillo's comments on the *modernista* drama. This particular issue probably contributed much to the general interest in the subject of wandering circus performers at the Quatre Gats *tertulia*, notably among the younger members, Opisso and Picasso.

Articles that appeared in 1899, the first year of publication, included coverage of exhibitions, among them the major Casas retrospective that was sponsored in October by the editors of *Pèl & Ploma* at the Sala Parés. Significant attention was also paid to related events in Paris, including official exhibitions, gallery shows, cabaret and café entertainment, and comments on individual painters. The *Pèl & Ploma* staff frequently reviewed European periodicals, such as *L'Art décoratif* and *La Plume*, which included illustrations by Beardsley, Fantin-Latour, Anquetin,

Willette, Toulouse-Lautrec, and many others. In 1900 considerable attention was paid to the Exposition Universelle in Paris held that year, which attracted so many of the younger generation of Els Quatre Gats, as a drawing by Picasso testifies [26].

The issues that appeared throughout 1900 were longer, and in several of the later numbers outstanding personalities in the world of arts and letters—Catalonians, Parisians, even Americans—were featured. Naturally, many of these figures were sympathetic to the *modernistas*. Normally Utrillo, using the pseudonym Pinzell, wrote a biographic study and Casas contributed a portrait drawing. This joint contribution alone accounts for *Pèl & Ploma*'s significance as an unusually valuable record of the *modernista* period.

Pèl & Ploma survived the life of Els Quatre Gats. There were memorable features on Toulouse-Lautrec (November 1901), Whistler (July 1903), and Gauguin (August 1903), and issues were also devoted to promising young artists, such as Picasso (June 1901). Publication was halted for six months from June to December in 1902, but resumed and continued throughout 1903. In the last issue of that year Utrillo included an announcement of a new magazine called *Forma*, which would replace *Pèl & Ploma*. The dispersal of the Quatre Gats group greatly affected the content of the new publication, which lasted until 1907. Feature articles were occasionally devoted to contemporary artists, but with time *Forma* increasingly took on the character of an art-historical journal, reflecting the changing interests of Utrillo and the disappearance of the café.

After the turn of the century, activities at Els Quatre Gats began to shift in favor of the younger group that gathered there. Although the original "four cats" were often present, they now comfortably pursued their own interests and in a sense functioned in a supervisory capacity. The year 1900 signalled not only the new century, but a new climate in Catalonia and at Els Quatre Gats.

The Year 1900

The actual turn of the century was marked at Els Quatre Gats with the installation of a painting by Casas to replace his earlier one of Romeu and himself on a tandem bicycle [10]. The 1897 composition thus became a farewell to the nineteenth century, symbolized by the bicycle, while the new work, Romeu and Casas in an automobile, signified progress and optimism in the twentieth century. In a photograph of the tavern interior (fig. 6) a portion of the new composition is seen at the upper left, placed in the same frame as the earlier work; among those seated at the tables is the proprietor Romeu at the far right. A drawing made by Ricardo Opisso (fig. 7), probably based upon a similar photograph, affords a more complete view of the new painting. At the table below, Opisso added an illustrious group of patrons, including (from left to right) Nonell, Junyer-Vidal, Picasso, Angel de Soto, Opisso, Canals, Vidal Ventosa, and Casagemas; Romeu is seated in the right foreground.

7 Ricardo Opisso. *Els Quatre Gats*, charcoal on paper, ca. 1900.
From left to right: Nonell, Junyer-Vidal, Picasso, Angel de Soto, Opisso, Canals,
Vidal Ventosa, Casagemas, and Romeu. Private collection

Events at the café in 1900 covered a broad range of artistic activities such as literary sessions, conferences, and musical performances. Although Quatre Gats was never considered to be a café concert (one that provides singing entertainment), a variety of musical performances were held there, apart from the piano accompaniment of the puppet theater. In 1900, for example, mentioned as guests at the café were Albéniz, Granados, Lluis Millet (all of whom had performed in Sitges), and in November the pianist Joaquín Nin gave one of his earliest recitals in Barcelona. In the same year, the respected Catalan poet Joan Maragall read his *Visions i cants* in a special session at the café.

The first exhibition at Els Quatre Gats in 1900, held in early February, featured one of the strongest personalities and most gifted artists to emerge from the younger group, Pablo Ruíz Picasso. Jaime Sabartés recalled in later years that the underlying motive for the show was to rival the almost exclusive reputation of Ramón Casas as a draftsman and portraitist.[23] Picasso included charcoal portraits of his Quatre Gats friends (*Portrait of Josef Cardona* [24] and *Portrait of Evelí Torent* [25] may have been among them), pastel sketches, and three oil paintings. The first review of the show in *La Vanguardia* mentioned only one of the oils and described it as the visit of a priest to a dying woman.[24] This painting, *The Dying Woman*, recently discovered by X-ray photographs beneath Picasso's *La Vie* (Cleveland Museum of Art), was the most ambitious work in the small exhibition.[25] The subject probably derived both from Picasso's own preoccupation with death in those years and from the *modernista* predilection for themes of illness, as in Rusiñol's *The Morphine Addict* [42], and evocative interiors, as in Casas's *Anxiety* [9].

Another Picasso exhibition was planned for 1900 in collaboration with his friend of several years, Manuel Pallarés. He and Pallarés had met at the Barcelona art academy La Llotja as students as early as 1895 and had spent time together at the Pallarés family home in Horta de San Juan during the summer of 1898. It was probably through Pallarés that Picasso was first introduced to the Quatre Gats group in that year. The planned show apparently was not realized and an unfinished poster project is the only remaining evidence of their intentions.[26]

The exhibition in March was of another non-Catalan artist, Carlos Vázquez, who was known in Madrid for his numerous magazine illustrations in journals such as *Blanco y Negro*. After taking up residence in Barcelona, he began, like his friend Picasso, to frequent Els Quatre Gats. Opisso wrote in *La Vanguardia* that the show "merits visiting, for it constitutes something of a demonstration of the currents which dominate in Paris . . . and influence the works exhibited by Vázquez."[27] Vázquez's subjects ranged from views of Paris, including a faithful depiction of an industrial zone along the Seine, to Spanish gardens. (In a later work of 1904 [50], Vázquez was to adapt a study by him of a Paris storefront so as to represent a Spanish one.) In general, Opisso characterized Vázquez's work as "romanticized" and somewhat narrative.

Still another exhibition is said to have occurred in March 1900, featuring the work of Picasso's friend and inseparable companion, Carles Casagemas.[28] Although no reviews of the show have been found, the works that were exhibited were probably charcoal and pastel drawings, such as *Landscape with Large Building* [5].

23 Jaime Sabartés, *Picasso: An Intimate Portrait*, New York, 1946, 54.
24 For the full text of Rodriguez Códola's review in *La Vanguardia* (3 Feb. 1900), see McCully, "Els Quatre Gats," 1975, appendix XXV.
25 A forthcoming article in the *Cleveland Museum of Art Bulletin* by Marilyn McCully and Robert McVaugh discusses the discovery of *The Dying Woman* and its implication for Picasso's early work.
26 Cirlot, *Picasso: el nacimiento de un genio*, no. 735.
27 Alfredo Opisso, "Exposición Carlos Vázquez," *La Vanguardia* (9 March 1900), 4.
28 Palau Fabre, *Picasso i els seus amics catalans*, 104.

Picasso and Els Quatre Gats

The importance of Els Quatre Gats for Picasso is a subject of considerable interest. The young artist produced a large body of work during this period, including a number of advertisements for Els Quatre Gats, and it was a crucial time in his artistic and emotional development. The support he found among an older, established generation of painters, as well as the camaraderie of his bohemian friends, provided Picasso with confidence at an early age that allowed for artistic experimentation. Artists such as Casas, Rusiñol, and Nonell made an impression on him and evidence of their influence can be found in his work of the period. Furthermore, a study of Picasso's oeuvre suggests that many of the themes that originated during the Barcelona years were returned to again and again by the artist in his later life.

Among the printed ephemera that Picasso created for Els Quatre Gats, the most popular was the 1899 menu cover *4 Gats: Menestra* (fig. 9). Another version of the front cover, with the word *menestra* ("food," in colloquial usage) omitted, was circulated as a small flyer for café publicity.[29] On the back cover was a portrait of Pere Romeu; in the example from Picasso's own collection that is reproduced here, Picasso drew caricatures over the printed image.

29 Palau Fabre, *Picasso en Cataluña*, no. 51.

The front cover depicts a group of fashionable clients seated at café tables set up on the Pasaje de San José (see fig. 1). Behind them, and framing the central figures, is one of the gothic arches that characterize the brick exterior of the Casa Martí. The linear and spatial conception of this work is reminiscent of English and American art-nouveau designs by artists such as Beardsley and Bradley and reflects Picasso's awareness of the international style. Although simple, flat shapes predominate—the woman and her fancy little dog, for example, are enclosed with one outline —a freer drawing style is also incorporated. The heavy lines in the opening of the arch, for example, produce a dark shadow and the cross-hatching of the foreground figure's trousers conveys a textured effect. The overall result is particularly charming, and the distinctive lettering contributes to the image of an attractive, cosmopolitan café.

A related announcement (fig. 10), printed on inexpensive paper and used as a handout, shows a woman approaching Els Quatre Gats, looking back over her shoulder before she joins the crowd at the entrance. The bouquet she carries indicates that she may be a flower seller. Judging from the presence of children among the group of figures, this was probably intended to publicize the *putxinel-lis* event. Picasso made no attempt here to alter his drawing technique with flattened shapes or linear patterns. The resulting quality of this little advertisement, which was printed in black on colored paper, is that of an original sketch.

Picasso also created an extremely clever menu design in about 1900 (fig. 11), although it is not known that the design was ever printed. The pastel drawing represents a waiter holding a sign *Plat del dia* in one hand and a bottle of wine in the other. On either side of his head is the lettering *4 Gats* and below is an empty frame for the addition of a handwritten "daily special." Romeu attempted to push the restaurant aspect of the establishment in 1900 and special prices and dishes, such as *tripa a la catalana* or *bacalao a la viscaina*, were often, although irregularly, publicized in local papers. Josep Pla reported that Romeu was a

rather haphazard administrator and for that reason
one could not always count on the restaurant to
provide adequate meals.[30]

One large-scale drawing from 1902 that was either
used as a poster itself or was designed for reproduction was *Pere Romeu—4 gats* [30]. This pencil drawing contrasts in technique and in the message conveyed with the earlier menu cover, *4 Gats: Menestra*
(fig. 9). In both designs Picasso presents a group of
individuals who might be expected to be found at Els
Quatre Gats. But the fashionable, elegant clientele of
the earlier drawing has been replaced by a group of
artists whose Barcelona reputation was associated
with Romeu's establishment (Romeu appears at the

left), notably Picasso himself in bohemian attire in the
left foreground. The rapid drawing tends to focus on
the individual personalities of the group and creates
great linear variation. The rendering of the dog, for
example, is independently active and not confined to
the decorative outline pattern as in the earlier design.
The drawing reflects not only the extraordinary
facility Picasso had developed as a draftsman by 1902
but also the changing appeal of Els Quatre Gats. The
older group of *modernista* artists, with the exception
of Romeu, had been replaced by Picasso and his
friends, who had become the attraction and moti-
vating force of café life.

Two of Picasso's last Quatre Gats projects, specifically made for Romeu, were a printed announcement of the birth of Romeu's son in 1902 and a New

30 Pla, *Santiago Rusiñol y su tiempo*, 230.

Year's card for 1903 based on the same drawing (fig. 12).[31] In the card, to the left of the drawing of the child, is a greeting that reads in translation: "Perico Romeu, little *hostaler* of Els Quatre Gats, in his name and on behalf of his parents, wishes you a happy 1903." Among Picasso's numerous drawings from this period, additional ideas for unexecuted café publicity can also be found.[32]

Following Picasso's exhibition at Els Quatre Gats in 1900, a more important show of his work was sponsored at the Sala Parés by the editors of *Pèl & Ploma* in 1901. Included were pastels from Picasso's

first trip to Paris and charcoal drawings from Málaga.[33] To celebrate the exhibition and Picasso's return to Barcelona (from Paris, Málaga, and Madrid), he was the featured artist in the June 1901 issue of *Pèl & Ploma*. A portrait by Casas and a short biography by Utrillo accompanied the reproduction of several Picasso drawings. Utrillo's article traces the artistic development of the "little Goya," as he had been called in Paris, and, significantly, initiates one of the longest and most consistently favorable bibliographies in art history. It was this kind of support from the Quatre Gats group that aided Picasso in making the decision to expand his artistic opportunities beyond Spain's borders and, after Els Quatre Gats closed, to move permanently to Paris.

31 Palau Fabre, *Picasso en Cataluña*, no. 72. The birth announcement reads: *Na Corina y En Pere Romeu (Hostalers dels Quatre Gats) es complauren en ferli á saber el naixement del primer fill (12 Maig 1902). Pere Romeu Jáuregui. padri: Esteve Huguet, padrina: Josefa Malagá.*

32 See, for example, Daix 1.2.

33 See, for example, Maragall, *Història de la Sala Parés*, no. 64.

Picasso's Debt to Modernismo

The more complex question of influences on Picasso's work during the Barcelona years must also be considered, for it was Picasso's habit to study the work of other artists, both older and contemporary, and to incorporate aspects of their techniques and subjects into his own developing style. Els Quatre Gats, as the center of *modernista* activities in Barcelona at the turn of the century, thus provided Picasso with exposure to new Catalan art and to artistic theories from outside of Spain as well.

The presence of Ramón Casas at the café was of special importance to the draftsmen of the group, who were intent on rendering every aspect of life around them. Casas's exhibition of 132 charcoal and pencil portraits at the Sala Parés in his important retrospective show, "Una iconografía barcelonina," held in October 1899, drew attention to the medium of charcoal (instead of the more traditional oil on canvas) and to Casas's characteristic, rapid technique. Picasso's own show just a few months later, held at Els Quatre Gats, reflected both his admiration for Casas's portraiture and the rivalry he and the younger

group felt for the older, established artist.

Picasso's adaptation of certain stylistic devices he found in the work of Casas is worth noting. An example is Picasso's 1901 portrait of his early patron in Paris, the Catalan industrialist Pere Manyac (fig. 13). The figure is contained by a heavily painted contour line, accentuating the light areas of his shirt and the cut-out shape formed by the bent elbow at the left. Although an oil on canvas, the work suggests a poster-like conception and comparison may be made to a similar technique in Casas's painting of Romeu and himself on a tandem bicycle [10], which hung in the tavern interior until 1900. In this work, Casas simplified the huge image, which actually functioned as a mural decoration and thus in a sense as a large-scale poster, and allowed the black contour line to animate the drawing. A hint of the Barcelona skyline (Montjuich at the right) is also conveyed through a single line. The same strong outline was used by Casas in individual painted portraits, such as his undated *Portrait of Romeu* wearing a Catalan *barretina* hat (fig. 14).

13 Pablo Picasso. *Portrait of Manyac*,
oil on canvas, 1901.
Chester Dale Collection, National Gallery of Art,
Washington, D.C.

14 Ramón Casas. *Portrait of Romeu*, oil on canvas.
Private collection

Comparison of this with Picasso's portrait of Manyac serves to illustrate the essential differences between the two artists, although at first glance the paintings seem quite alike. Both indeed present a figure that fills the space of the canvas and is surrounded by essentially flat color. The heavily painted contour line accentuates the posture in each case, and in so doing conveys a suggestion of the sitter's personality. Manyac, a large powerful man, is portrayed full-face and upright, exuding self-confidence; Romeu, on the other hand, slightly slouched, seems more introspective. The comparison also points up the more daring, and at the same time humorous, attitude Picasso takes towards form. The use of a few simple strokes in the face conveys Manyac's particular features and also echoes the larger treatment of the body. The cleverly painted tie is really a brush stroke overlapping the white paint of the flattened shirt. The placement of the hands, also reduced to simplified brush strokes, accentuates the enormous size of Picasso's patron. Because of these departures from Casas's technique by Picasso, the Romeu portrait seems the more naturalistic of the two.

Thematically, Picasso probably owes more to Rusiñol and Nonell during the Quatre Gats period than to Casas. Certainly the *modernista* woman, portraits of friends, and places of entertainment appear in Picasso's Barcelona work, and reflect in part the popularization of these subjects by Casas. Perhaps the real significance of Casas's thematic contribution to Picasso, particularly in the scenes of Parisian life, is that Picasso went to Casas's own sources when he traveled to Paris, to the work of artists such as Degas and Toulouse-Lautrec.

Picasso and many of the other young members of the Quatre Gats group shared an interest in themes dealing with the poor and unfortunate ranks of society. The subject reflects the *modernista* insistence on recording real life first developed by Rusiñol and Casas in the early 1890s, and continued by artists such as Nonell and Canals in the mid-1890s. A work such as *End of the Road* by Picasso (fig. 15) thus functions at once as a statement on social conditions and as an allegory of death; in both respects the work relates to *modernista* themes. The painting depicts two separate processions winding up a hillside to a cemetery where, as Picasso explained years later, "Death waits for all at the end of the road, even though the rich go there in carriages and the poor on foot."[34] Comparison of *End of the Road* and Nonell's earlier *Annunciation in the Slums* [19] demonstrates the similarity of thematic concern yet the difference of intent of the two artists. In the Nonell drawing, the angel appears as a vision, bringing glad tidings to the incredulous group of poor and demented creatures who inhabit the slums and for whom there is no hope—it is a false illusion. For Picasso, the rich and poor alike meet the angel of death at the end of the road of life—it is a universal message, the truth. Nonell's sardonic statement is thus contrasted by Picasso's compassionate irony.

The transformation of the scene in *End of the Road* into allegory also suggests the symbolist suggestion and imaginative imagery of *modernista* illustration, represented by artists such as Pichot [36], whose women meet the monsters of their dreams. In addition, a figure of death similar to that in *End of the Road* occurs in at least one of Picasso's drawings of

this period (*Dead Girl*, Museo Picasso, Barcelona), in which it hovers over the young woman's deathbed.[35] This drawing, a preparatory sketch for *The Dying Woman*, the large painting Picasso exhibited in his first Quatre Gats exhibition in 1900, suggests that *End of the Road* may also relate to the subject of that work.

Finally, the more subtle and perhaps more important influence of Rusiñol on the early work of Picasso must also be considered. Picasso's friendship with Rusiñol and his first-hand knowledge of Rusiñol's painting, both at Els Quatre Gats and in Sitges, gave him the opportunity to consider the implications of Rusiñol's conception of *modernista* painting. The special combination of an approach based upon naturalism, drawing subjects from the real world, and the evocation of mood or symbolism through painterly means was ultimately understood and developed by Picasso to a degree that surpassed that of Rusiñol and the other *modernista* painters at the turn of the century. For example, *Crouching Woman* of 1902 [31] does indeed reflect an interest in the subject of the tragedy of the poor and social alienation, found in works by other Spanish artists such as Nonell [20]. Yet, the real power of this painting and of the works of Picasso's Blue Period in general lies in his use of formal means to convey mood. The crowded space of the hunched figure, withdrawn and self-contained in her empty ambiguous setting, enhanced by the dominant blue of Picasso's limited palette, evokes the sorrow of her social isolation. It is this particular combination of factors—subjects drawn from the humblest ranks of society and the power of the painted image to convey universal as well as personal statements about the condition of life—that Picasso took from *modernismo*, reinterpreted, and developed into the personal vocabulary that characterized his work through 1905.

34 John Richardson, *Picasso: Watercolours and Gouaches*, London, 1964, 16.

35 *Joven muerta*, Museo Picasso (MAB 110.750); Cirlot, *Picasso: el nacimiento de un genio*, no. 199.

The Decline of Els Quatre Gats

By 1903 the character of Els Quatre Gats had changed considerably. The *modernista* artists had begun to disperse, many had gone to Paris, and a new wave of painting, a shift to a more classicizing form and content, started to emerge in Barcelona. In March 1903 three artists new to the Quatre Gats group—Manel Ainaud, Enric Casanovas, and Claudi Grau—exhibited drawings in the *sala gran* and critics noted the stylistic change represented by their work.[36] While their subjects still reflected the *modernista* interest in daily life, the sketchy quality of drawings in the nineties had given way to a stronger and more academic definition.

At the end of March, the young writer Jaime Sabartés (1881–1968) delivered a series of literary evenings at Els Quatre Gats and his contribution was the last announced function of the café. Jacobus Sabartés, as he advertised himself at the time, had been a regular patron from at least 1899, when his friend Picasso had begun to make portraits of him. In the *sala gran* of Els Quatre Gats Sabartés read his prose and verse, and although he and his friends thought of him as a decadent poet, the *La Vanguardia* reviewer who attended the sessions claimed that Sabartés would never arrive in those diffuse regions of the "land of dreams," so strong was his grasp on reality.[37]

The actual closing of Els Quatre Gats in July 1903 was uneventful, a good indication of the loss of the fervor that had characterized it in earlier years. The actual space in the Puig i Cadafalch building was next leased to another group of artists, the strictly regionalist Circol Artistich de Sant Lluch. They moved into the Casa Martí and installed themselves in remodeled rooms in January 1904. The new headquarters were inaugurated with an exhibition of paintings and sculpture by members of the conservative Circol—far away in spirit from the little exhibitions that had functioned as avant-garde manifestations in the recent past. The closing of Els Quatre Gats signalled the passing of a moment of intense artistic activity, a proud one in the history of Catalonia.

36 See, for example, Raimon Casellas, "Notas d'art," *La Veu de Catalunya* (19 March 1903).

37 "Jacobus Sabartés," *La Vanguardia* (31 March 1903), 3.

15 Pablo Picasso. *End of the Road,*
watercolor and conté crayon on paper, ca. 1899.
J. K. Thannhauser Collection,
Solomon R. Guggenheim Museum, New York

Chronology of Events at Els Quatre Gats

1897

JUNE Els Quatre Gats opens in Barcelona, advertised as a *cerveseria-taverna-hostal*.

JULY Inaugural exhibition, including works by Bonnin, Canals, Casas, Espert, Mir, Nonell, Pichot, Rusiñol, Torent, Utrillo.

DECEMBER *Sombras artísticas*, shadow puppet theater, under the direction of Utrillo is inaugurated as a regular feature. First program includes participation of Maragall, Morera, Utrillo, Jordà, Gay, Pichot, de Fuentes, and Casas.

1898

FEBRUARY New *sombras artísticas* program is presented with works by Vallmitjana, Bonnin, and Ginesta.

NOVEMBER *Putxinel-lis*, marionette theater, under the direction of Julio Pi is established as a regular feature. First individual exhibition is held in the *sala gran*, featuring Dario de Regoyos.

DECEMBER Isidro Nonell exhibition; Rubén Darío visits Els Quatre Gats.

1899

JANUARY La Sociedad Colómbofila meets at Els Quatre Gats.
A traveling exhibition of carnival posters from Vilanova i Geltrú is shown.
"Feline" literary competition is sponsored.

FEBRUARY Ramón Pichot exhibition.
The first issue of the journal *Quatre Gats* is published, under the direction of Utrillo, Casas, and Romeu. Tickets for bicycle races in the Jardines del Parque are sold at Els Quatre Gats.

APRIL Xavier Gosé exhibition.

MAY *Putxinel-lis* drama contest sponsored.

JUNE Evelí Torent exhibition.

JULY Josep Dalmau exhibition.

OCTOBER El Club Autonomista Català meets at Els Quatre Gats to hear speech entitled "Centre Democratich Federal."

DECEMBER Phonograph introduced by optician Eugenio Roselló at a session entitled "Edison: a great man."

1900

JANUARY Poster competition sponsored.

FEBRUARY Pablo Ruíz Picasso exhibition.

MARCH Carlos Vázquez exhibition.
Carles Casagemas exhibition.

NOVEMBER Piano recital given by Joaquín Nin.

1901

FEBRUARY A certain Papuss fasts for eight days at Els Quatre Gats to prove it can be done.

JUNE The Sisters Kokin (unidentified performers).

OCTOBER Agrupació Wagneriana (Wagner society) is formed at Els Quatre Gats.

1902

MARCH La Sociedad Cartofila Española *Hispania* (a group of print and postcard collectors) meets at Els Quatre Gats.

1903

MARCH Exhibition of drawings by Ainaud, Casanovas, Grau.
Jaime Sabartés reads his own works in evening sessions.

MAY Real Club de Barcelona meets at Els Quatre Gats.

JULY Els Quatre Gats closes.

Undated activities

EXHIBITIONS Ricardo Canals, Luisa Vidal, Ignacio Zuloaga, the Benlliure brothers: Blas, José, Mariano, José Antonio.

MUSIC Gay, Albéniz, Granados, Llobet.

SPECIAL GUESTS AND BANQUETS Vincent d'Indy, Miguel de los Santos Oliver, the Quintero brothers, Emilio Junoy, Carlos Costa, Réjane, Colonne, Antonio Ribera, La Duse.

Catalogue
of the
Exhibition

Hermen Anglada Camarasa
1873–1959

The painter Anglada Camarasa first studied at the Barcelona art academy La Llotja and also in the studio of Modest Urgell. He later completed his training in Paris with Jean-Paul Laurens and Benjamin Constant. In 1898 Anglada exhibited at the Société Nationale des Beaux Arts and was elected a member in 1902. Like many of the Barcelona group at the turn of the century, he worked between the two cities, principally in Paris. Picasso knew Anglada in Barcelona from the Quatre Gats days,[1] and their friendship continued in Paris, where both belonged to a Spanish group whose members saw each other during the years between 1905 and 1910. Anglada later moved to Mallorca, where he lived and painted until his death in Puerto de Pollensa (Mallorca) in 1959.

1 See Picasso's portrait of Anglada, Z.VI.119.

I   *Studies of a Dancer*

Among the five drawings, two are numbered 1; for purposes of identification these are here classified as 1 and 1a (the latter corresponds to the dancer facing left, who is drawn on an irregularly cut sheet). The signatures on all five drawings were added at a later date by a second hand as authentication. With the exception of no. 4 (in black crayon), the drawings are done in blue crayon and are probably all sketches of one particular dancer in performance. Line emphasizes movement, notably in the full skirts in motion; the various positions of the dark stockings are also given particular emphasis. With this economy of line, Anglada conveys the lively quality of an aspect of Parisian entertainment that attracted so many of the Quatre Gats group to its cafés, cabarets, and dance halls. In spirit these drawings recall similar sketches by Picasso from his first visits to Paris in the early 1900s.[1]

1 See, for example, Daix II.4.

Private collection

Ca. 1900; signed lower right: *H. Anglada Camarasa*.
Five drawings, crayon on paper;
(1) 12 x 14.3 cm; (1a) 8.9 x 12.1 cm;
(2) 10.2 x 13.4 cm; (3) 11.7 x 13.3 cm;
(4) 8.5 x 11.3 cm.

Provenance: Viuda de Anglada Camarasa.

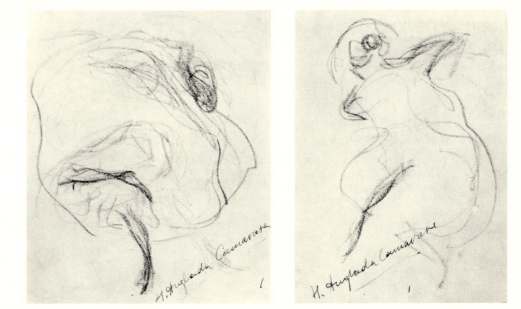

Lluis Bonnin Martí
1872–1935

Born in Barcelona, Bonnin received his earliest training in jewelry-making at the art academy La Llotja. During the 1890s his characteristically linear drawings were popular in journals such as *Barcelona Cómica*, *Catalonia*, and *Hispania*. Seven works by Bonnin, including an oil portrait, were shown in the first Quatre Gats exhibition in 1897. In 1900, Bonnin moved permanently to Nice, where he worked as a jeweler.

2 Illustrations for *Boires baixes* by Josep Maria Roviralta (A) Dream Woman at the Well / (B) The Wanderer / (C) Spirits Arming the Wanderer / (D) Hero at the Castle Door / (E) Old Woman and the Wanderer / (F) Dream Woman and the Tree of Love / (G) The Fountain / (H) Two Lovers

When *Boires baixes* ("*Rolling Mists*"), a Zarathustrian poem of dreams by Josep Maria Roviralta, appeared in 1902, Eugenio d'Ors recognized its hero as a personification of the *modernista* period.[1] With the musical accompaniment composed by Enrich Granados and a set of illustrations produced by Lluis Bonnin, the work is also characteristic of the period's enthusiasm for the *gesamtkunstwerk*. Bonnin's plates appeared in the limited first edition of the poem and were considered sufficiently important to merit an independent exhibition, which took place in May at Casa Josep Ribas. For the show the printer Oliva produced two hundred sets of plates, one of which is displayed here.

In the book the eight illustrative prints are interspersed in the text, which they roughly parallel. In the first, "Dream Woman at the Well," Bonnin provides a vision of the "woman/symbol" who serves as the poem's unattained ideal. In it, he also establishes the setting of the dream's action with its enclosing forest, barely discernible castle, and the well. In the early portion of the text the dream woman appears only briefly in a vision (14), and consequently Bonnin's plate must be considered as a visual introduction akin to the songs she sings early in the poem. The second illustration, "The Wanderer," serves to introduce the poem's protagonist. Here Bonnin concentrates on the figure alone, to the total exclusion of the setting. The same nervous energy characterizes the first two plates, but in "The Wanderer," Bonnin's stroke is broader, more fluid, and the image is less cluttered. In "Spirits Arming the Wanderer," Bonnin returns to a denser image in which figures and environment tend to merge in a morass of line. The setting is similar to that of "Dream Woman at the Well," although now the castle gate is more prominent and the region is thickly overgrown. This plate, unlike its predecessors, directly illustrates the section of the poem in which Imagination calls on the spirits to provide the Wanderer with armor,

Private collection

1902; signed in plates: *Ll. Bonnin*. *Tirage à part*, consisting of eight unnumbered etchings, issued in paper wrapper with title page and additional printed leaves, and a mounted lithograph version of the first etching (A), one of 200 sets; (A, B, D, F, and H) 21.8 x 15.4 cm, (C and E) 15.4 x 21.8 cm, (G) 21.8 x 30.8 cm.

Provenance: Josep Canudas; Libreria Porter, Barcelona.

Bibliography: Roviralta, Josep Maria, *Boires baixes*, Vilanova i Geltrú, 1902, opp. 8 (A), opp. 16 (B), opp. 18 (C), opp. 22 (D), opp. 48 (E), opp. 56 (F), after 56 (G), opp. 72 (H); *Pèl & Ploma*, no. 85 (Feb. 1902), cover (A); Cirici, *El arte modernista catalán*, cover and 397 (H), 44 (D), 53 (G), 64 (F), 396 (A) as cover of *Pèl & Ploma* (Feb. 1902); Blunt and Pool, *Picasso*, no. 29 (H); Cervera, *Modernismo*, ill. 153 (F); Jardí, *Història de Els 4 Gats*, 17 (B), 32 (C and E), 33 (D and G), 92 (H), 154 (F).

Exhibition: Casa Josep Ribas, Barcelona, 1902.

1 Cirici, *El arte modernista catalán*, 54.

transforming him into the hero (22). Once armed, he approaches his goal, and in the fourth illustration, "Hero at the Castle Door," we find him at the entrance despite the opposition of two fog-spirits swirling about him. To his surprise an old woman in black, Experience, opens the door instead of his dream woman. In the ensuing confrontation, Experience dissuades him from his pursuit of the woman in the castle. He departs, disarmed by her sober advice, as is shown in the next print, "Old Woman and the Wanderer." Though it does not directly illustrate any part of the text, it suggests their confrontation and her ultimate victory. In the sixth illustration, "Dream Woman and the Tree of Love," Bonnin returns to the text. The Ideal, coming out of the castle after the wanderer's departure, stands beneath the Tree of Love, which has grown from a flower he had previously cut. The blossoms and leaves fall through the fog around her, for the poem's combined love and seasonal cycle moves into its autumnal phase (57). "The Fountain," which immediately follows "Dream Woman and the Tree of Love" in the book, has no direct textual source. In it, numerous fog-spirits hover about and gaze into the well, in the midst of which a fountain rises, topped by a human face. Although the entire dream narrative has taken place at night, it is only in this print that the chill and weight of the darkness intrude. The final plate, "Two Lovers," does not depict the hero/wanderer and the dream woman, for their union was prevented by the voice of Experience. The two lovers here must be the dream woman and the man of genius over whom the song of the spirit rather than the voice of reason holds sway (67). The allusion to genius lends added significance to the choice of this design for a vignette printed on one of the extra leaves in the *tirage à part*, above the initials of the three collaborators, Roviralta, Bonnin, and Granados (see illustration).

The visual character of the eight illustrations varies greatly. "The Wanderer" is the simplest image, limited to the single profile figure and broadly sketched. Only "Two Lovers" is similarly devoid of setting and it differs markedly from "The Wanderer" in the attenuated elegance of its line and its studied integrity as an image. In contrast, "The Fountain," "Spirits Arming the Wanderer," and "Old Woman and the Wanderer," present cluttered visual environments in which figures and objects are submerged in the system of interweaving lines. "Dream Woman at the Well," "Hero at the Castle Door," and "Dream Woman and the Tree of Love" stand between the extreme of pictorial density and simplicity noted above. A Northern spirit, related to Maeterlinckian silence and early romantic *märchen*, pervades the poem and its illustrations. The imagery is primarily medieval, with one notable exception, for the "Two Lovers" employs renaissance imagery stemming from Bonnin's enthusiasm for the work of Benvenuto Cellini.

Plate D: "Hero at the Castle Door"

Plate F: "Dream Woman and the Tree of Love"

Plate E: "Old Woman and the Wanderer"

The prints relate to a style of illustration developed largely in England, which was well known in Barcelona through imported publications such as *Studio*. Resemblances to Charles Robinson's fussy illustrations for Gabriel Setoun's collection of poems, *Child's World* (1896) are strong. A distinguishing aspect of Bonnin's technique, particularly evident in the denser plates, is his use of short hatching lines. They appear most frequently in the definition of human figures, where, in their association with volumetric representation, they often disturb the pictorial integrity of the plates. Moreover, they suggest weight in the figures, which directly contradicts the floating, almost aquatic impression conveyed by many of the prints.

The cover for the *tirage à part* includes two distinct styles of graphic design. The repeating terns moving across the top are depicted with a crisp geometric regularity which, along with the choice of lettering, suggests a German rather than English source. On the back cover, however, this regularity is disturbed by a slightly altered version of the "Two Lovers," who stand on the outstretched wings of a stylized owl. The juxtaposition of the swirling, linear lovers and the stable, planar bird reflects the enthusiasm for the irrational, the pursuit of which in dreams is a cornerstone of the poem itself. R.M.

Ricardo Canals Llambí
1876–1931

After a short enrollment at the art academy La Llotja, Ricardo Canals joined his classmates Nonell and Joaquim Mir and formed the Colla de Sant Martí, a group dedicated to painting out of doors and taking everyday life as their subject. Canals made his first trip to Paris in 1897 in the company of Nonell. Together they exhibited there at the gallery Le Barc de Boutteville in 1898 as part of the "Quinzième Exposition des Peintres Impressionistes et Symbolistes." As one of the original group that met at Els Quatre Gats, Canals included five drawings in the first exhibition there in 1897. Works by Canals were also shown in New York at the Durand Ruel galleries in 1902. After Canals's association with the Quatre Gats ended, he lived in Madrid and Seville and in 1906 returned to Paris. Canals's early interest in social themes, particularly lower-class Spanish life, gave way to a preference for portraiture in his later years.

3   *Café Concert*
       Café concierto; *La revista*

This very loosely painted and colorful composition depicts a line of dancers seen from a high tier in the audience. From this vantage point Canals includes the viewer among the crowd of spectators to the right of the composition. The orchestra occupies an intermediate position and the silhouetted bass fiddler at the left links this section two-dimensionally to the illuminated stage. Canals certainly owes his general theme, the device of the spectators' point of view, and the bass fiddle motif to late-nineteenth-century painting, made popular by artists such as Degas in France and Casas in Spain, in such works as the latter's *Dance at the Moulin de la Galette* [6]. In mood, however, the composition still relates to Canals's own lively Spanish café interiors, usually of lower-class entertainment, of the 1890s.[1]

1 See, for example, *Danseuses espagnoles* in Barcelona, *Ricardo Canals*, no. 17.

Museo de Arte Moderno, Barcelona

Ca. 1903; signed upper right: *Canals*. Oil on canvas; 50 x 65.8 cm.

Provenance: Sala Parés; Barbey Collection; Santiago Espona; acquired in 1958.

Bibliography: Pujols, "A la memòria de Ricard Canals en ocasió de una exposició d'homenatge," *Mirador* (16 March 1933), ill. 215; Cirici, *El arte modernista catalán*, 369; Larco, *La pintura española moderna y contemporánea*, vol. 3, ill. 216 (as *Escena en teatro*); *Blanco y Negro* (1 Nov. 1969), no. 3000; Gaya Nuño, *La pintura española del siglo XX*, 109; Maragall, *Història de la Sala Parés*, ill. 115.

Exhibitions: Sala Parés, Barcelona, 1933, "Homenatge a Ricard Canals," no. 6; Salon Tinell, Barcelona, 1958, "Legado Espona," no. 123; Casón de Buen Retiro, Madrid, 1962, "Exposición de pintura catalana desde la prehistoria hasta nuestros dias"; Palacio de la Virreina, Barcelona, 1955, "Pujols y los artistas de su tiempo," no. 29; Museo de Arte Moderno, Barcelona, 1976.

4 *Self-Portrait*

The inscription on the back of the canvas, by Canals's friend Vázquez Díaz, witnesses that he saw Canals paint this self-portrait in Paris in 1906. Although it dates from the post-Quatre Gats period, the work demonstrates Canals's fine handling of paint and his concern for form. The direction of the brush strokes of the thickly applied paint gives a sense of texture and three-dimensionality, particularly in the area of the nose and temples of the well-defined head. Canals's preference at this date for portraiture and the human figure, without the social overtones of his work from the 1890s, relates to a similar shift of focus in the work of his friend Nonell (whose models are predominantly gypsies after 1900) and to a fondness for French painters, such as Renoir and Cézanne.

Establecimientos Maragall, S.A., Barcelona (25.927)

1906; inscribed, signed, and dated on verso: *Autorretrato de Ricardo Canals, visto pintar, Paris, 1906, Vázquez Díaz.* Oil on canvas: 54 x 38 cm.

Provenance: Daniel Vázquez Díaz, Madrid.

Bibliography: Larco, *La pintura española moderna y contemporánea,* vol. 2, 22; Socias, Jaume, *Canals,* Barcelona, 1976, 156.

Exhibitions: Sala Parés, Barcelona, 1975, *Epoca del Sr. Parés,* no. 5; Museo de Arte Moderno, Barcelona, 1976, *Ricardo Canals,* no. 30; Sala Parés, Barcelona, 1977.

Carles Casagemas Coll
1880–1901

Carles Casagemas first began his artistic studies with the set designer Felix Urgèlles in Barcelona. Afterwards the young Casagemas turned to drawing and writing and contributed poems to Barcelona journals, such as *Quatre Gats* and *Joventut*. His studio on the Carrer Nou in Barcelona became something of an artistic salon for the younger members of the Quatre Gats group, who met there on Sunday afternoons and included such individuals as Vidal Ventosa, Nonell, and occasionally Picasso.[1] Casagemas's first exhibition at Els Quatre Gats followed his friend Picasso's in 1900. Later in that year the two traveled to Paris, where they stayed in Nonell's apartment and visited the Exposition Universelle; a Picasso drawing *Leaving the Exposition Universelle* [26] is a record of this visit. After Casagemas suffered an unhappy love affair in Paris, the two artists returned to Spain. In spite of Picasso's efforts to cheer his friend, who had fallen into deep depression, Casagemas returned to Paris alone and in 1901 committed suicide.

1 Palau Fabre, *Picasso i els seus amics catalans*, 105.

5   *Landscape with Large Building*
      Paisaje con gran edificio

Landscape with Large Building is one of the small number of known drawings by Casagemas, whose artistic production was limited to a few short years. The drawing shows a dark landscape with a building in the distance and several trees in the foreground in tones of green. Casagemas conveys the sensation of evening through a combination of charcoal and the glowing quality of the yellow paper beneath. The compositional division and mood of this drawing suggest the pastel by Picasso from about 1899, *Burial in the Country* (Museo Picasso, Barcelona, MAB 110.233), a preparatory work for *End of the Road* (fig. 15).

Cau Ferrat, Sitges

Ca. 1899; signed upper right: *C. Casagemas*.
Charcoal and colored chalk on yellow paper; 26.6 x 34.8 cm.

Bibliography: Sitges, *Catálogo de pintura y dibujo del "Cau Ferrat,"* 14–15.

Ramón Casas Carbó
1866–1932

Casas's earliest artistic training in his native Barcelona was in the studio of the portrait painter and decorator Joan Vicens Cots. In 1882 Casas moved to Paris and entered the atelier of Carolus Duran; in 1884 he attended classes at the Académie Gervex. In 1890 he moved to Rusiñol's Moulin de la Galette apartment and began a rich collaboration with Rusiñol on a variety of projects, including the illustrations for *Desde el molino*, which appeared in *La Vanguardia* during the early 1890s. During this period Casas exhibited regularly in Barcelona and Paris, and by the turn of the century had established himself as a portraitist and poster designer. As artistic editor of *Pèl & Ploma*, Casas had numerous drawings of his own appear in that journal and in other Barcelona publications throughout the Quatre Gats years. Thirteen works by Casas were included in the first Quatre Gats exhibition, and his regular presence at the café was of great importance to the younger artists who gathered there. After the closing of Els Quatre Gats, Casas collaborated on various Barcelona publications and worked as a portraitist in the Catalan capital, Madrid, and in the United States. In 1916 his American friend Charles Deering, who owned many of his works [8, 16, 17] asked him to direct the decoration of Deering's castle at Tamarit (near Tarragona), where a studio was set up for Casas in the guest house. In Casas's later years, he alternated his residence between San Benito de Bages and Barcelona, where he died in 1932.

6 *Dance at the Moulin de la Galette*
Baile en el Moulin de la Galette; Sur la Butte

The fame of the Montmartre dance hall, the Moulin de la Galette, came from the lively dances, such as *le chahut*, that were done there. In Casas's painting, however, the dance and the mood it creates are unexpected. The actual dance occupies only a quarter of the composition in the lower left-hand section. Even then, there is only a small amount of movement among the dancers, who are silhouetted and flattened; the two dancing women (the figure at the left in the foreground and the other facing her at the far end of the dance floor) suggest the only evident motion, which is simply the raising of their skirts. Occupying most of the remaining space are the figures seated in double rows beneath the musicians' gallery and at the back, the ceiling and the hanging chandeliers, the very high band of windows providing the only source of light, and, finally, the orchestra.

The viewer, who sees the action from above, is on the same level as the rather ambiguous orchestra. With the exception of the conductor, the musicians are obscured by darkness and almost impossible to see. Instead, their presence is suggested by the musical instruments, particularly the neck of the bass fiddle which is silhouetted against the bright window. It is not at all unlikely that Casas was attracted by this motif in the work of Degas

Cau Ferrat, Sitges

1890; signed lower right: *R. Casas.*
Oil on canvas; 100 x 81.5 cm.

Bibliography: *Morning Post*, London, 1891, see Archivo Rusiñol, vol. 1, 66; *La Veu de Catalunya* (6 Dec. 1891); *Pèl & Ploma* (26 May 1900), 4, no. 51; *La Veu de Catalunya* (7 June 1900); *Joventut* (14 June 1900), 281–82; *Pèl & Ploma* (1 July 1900), 7; *Pèl & Ploma*, vol. 4 (1903), 32–33; Utrillo, "L'obra d'en Casas," 316; Jordà, *Ramón Casas, pintor*, 23, pl. 19; Sitges, *Guía del Museo del "Cau Ferrat" de Sitges*, 1940, 55; Sitges, *Catálogo de pintura y dibujo del "Cau Ferrat,"* 15; Sitges, *Guía sumaria del Cau Ferrat*, 66; Ráfols, José F., "La sinceridad en nuestra pintura de fin de siglo," *Anales y boletín de los museos de arte de Barcelona*, vol. 1–2 (Winter 1942), 11; Pla, *Santiago Rusiñol y su tiempo*, 110; Ráfols, *Modernismo y modernistas*, ill. 13; Ráfols, "Ramón Casas," 346–48; Ráfols, *Ramón Casas, pintor*, 15, 34, pl. 11; Jardí, Enric, *L'art català contemporani*, Barcelona, 1972, 62; Figuerola-Ferretti, Luis, "El arte en Madrid," *Goya*, no. 122 (Sept.–Oct. 1974), 113; McCully, "Els Quatre Gats," 1975, 150–52, ill. 18; Cervera, *Modernismo*, ill. 49.

Exhibitions: Salon des Indépendants, Paris, 1891; Salon de Champ de Mars, Paris, 1891, no. 168; Sala Parés, Barcelona, 1891; Sala Parés, Barcelona, 1900; Palacio de la Virreina, Barcelona, 1958, *Exposición Ramón Casas*, no. 122; Museo de Arte Moderno, Barcelona, 1974, *El impresionismo en España*, no. 13.

or Toulouse-Lautrec, who used the instrument in similar manner in their depictions of the café concert. In addition to this motif and to the general subject of the picture, other elements suggest Casas's indebtedness to the two French painters: the high, distanced point of view, so characteristic of Degas; and the flattening of the figures to create a silhouetted effect, made familiar by Toulouse-Lautrec.

The overall feeling evoked by this painting of a typical Parisian dance hall—where the dance was often considered wild or even scandalous—is strangely subdued, almost melancholy. The absence of any suggestion of gaiety of movement or facial expression, the separation of light from the action, and the removed point of view suggest isolation and psychological distance among the figures. Moreover, the technical execution complements this mood, for a loosened brush stroke animates the floor rather than the dancing figures. The brightest spots on the canvas are a glistening ceiling above the action and the accents of light, which are reflected in the mirrors on the lower level at the back.

7 Open Air Café
Plein Air

Casas submitted *Open Air Café*, a composition painted in Paris, to Barcelona's first Exposición General de Bellas Artes, from which it was acquired by the city. The subject is a woman seated at a café table out of doors near the entrance to the Moulin de la Galette, where a man is seen looking beyond the gate. Their presence in the misty atmospheric setting is enigmatic, and the mood is silent and chilly. The normal activity or life of the café is abruptly cut off by the central placement of the tables and chairs in the open space of the foreground. The fragmentation of the closest chair tends to flatten the upper part of it and confuse the chair's proportion in favor of its compositional function, suggesting that Casas may have taken this motif from Degas or Toulouse-Lautrec, in whose work the same device occurs.

The hazy quality of the background, in which the late afternoon lights glow above the Moulin de la Galette entrance, is reminiscent of the background setting of Casas's *Portrait of Erik Satie* [8]. This mistiness and ephemeral tonality indicate mood, in addition to the time of day and season of the year. The quality of atmospheric suggestion and the thin layers of paint that convey it recall similar effects in canvases by contemporary painters such as Whistler and Sargent, whose works Casas is likely to have known in Paris.

Museo de Arte Moderno, Barcelona

Ca. 1890–91; signed lower right: *R. Casas.*
Oil on canvas; 51 x 66 cm.

Provenance: acquired in 1891.

Bibliography: *La Vanguardia* (18 June 1891); *Pèl & Ploma* (26 May 1900), 4, no. 50; *Pèl & Ploma* (1 Nov. 1900), 5; *Catálogo del Museo de Bellas Artes*, Barcelona, 1906, 32; Casellas, *Etapes esètiques*, 78; *Catálogo del Museo de Arte Contemporáneo*, Barcelona, 1926, 149; Jordà, *Ramón Casas, pintor*, 25, pl. 11; Ráfols, "Les obres pictòriques de Casas al Museu de Barcelona," *Butlletí dels museus d'art de Barcelona*, 1932, 341–42; Ráfols, José F., "La sinceridad en nuestra pintura de fin de siglo," *Anales y boletín de los museos de arte de Barcelona*, vol. 1–2 (Winter 1942), 11; Ráfols, *Modernismo y modernistas*, ill. 12; Ráfols, *Ramón Casas, pintor*, 14–15, pl. 10; Cirici, *El arte modernista catalán*, 344; Pla, Josep, "Un conocido Ramón Casas," *Destino* (21 June 1969), 58; Gaya Nuño, *La pintura española del siglo XX*, 61, 66; Garrut, *Dos siglos de pintura catalana (XIX–XX)*, 224; McCully, "Els Quatre Gats," 1975, 153–54, ill. 19; Cervera, *Modernismo*, ill. 51.

Exhibitions: Barcelona, 1891, "Exposición General de Bellas Artes," no. 118; Sala Parés, Barcelona, 1900; Sala Parés, Barcelona, 1954, *Quatre Gats, Primer Salon "Revista,"* 40; Madrid, 1956, *Un siglo de arte español, 1856–1956*, 91, pl. 39; Palacio de la Virreina, Barcelona, 1958, *Exposición Ramón Casas*, no. 130; Museo de Arte Moderno, Barcelona, 1974, *El impresionismo en España*, no. 12.

8 *Portrait of Erik Satie*
El bohemio; Poet of Montmartre

The French composer Erik Satie (1866–1925) was a local Montmartre personality in the nineties and occasional pianist at Le Chat Noir. He began to perform regularly in about 1890 at the Auberge du Clou on the Avenue Trudaine and there, in 1891, he met Miguel Utrillo, who had set up a shadow puppet theater in the basement of the Auberge that year. In his "Història anecdòtica del Cau Ferrat," Utrillo recalled the day he brought Satie to the Moulin de la Galette in order to meet Rusiñol and Casas. Utrillo described the young musician as a smiling, pallid character with long blonde hair and a moustache, dressed that day in a jacket and trousers the color of *café au lait*, which had once belonged to an official of the Zouaves. Satie amused his new friends by improvising a "poor mass" on an old harmonium that he had found in the Catalans' apartment. At the urging of Rusiñol, Casas soon afterwards painted this large-scale portrait of Satie, dressed in the fashion of a Montmartre bohemian—hence the original title of *El bohemio*—standing in front of the Moulin de la Galette.

The paint is quite thinly applied and an underlying grid, which shows in the lower third of the canvas, suggests that Casas transferred a preliminary drawing for the final version. *Pentimenti* behind the figure show that Satie originally held an open umbrella.[1] In a drawing published in *La Vanguardia* (18 March 1892), Satie is holding a closed umbrella at his side. Several other sketches relate specifically to the work, although it is difficult to ascertain whether they were all preliminary to the painting. One, for example, may postdate it, for the problem Casas encountered with the angle of Satie's foot in the painting is resolved in the drawing by the extension of the shadow beneath it (fig. 16).[2]

1 I am grateful to Robert Lafond for pointing this out to me.
2 There is a more schematic version of fig. 16 in the Museo de Arte Moderno, Barcelona, no. 1063.

Northwestern University Library, Evanston, Illinois

1891; signed lower right: *R. Casas*. Oil on canvas; 198.8 x 99.7 cm; recently restored.

Provenance: Charles Deering; gift of Mrs. Chauncy McCormick in 1956.

Bibliography: *Morning Post* (London, 1891), see Archivo Rusiñol, vol. 1, 66; *La Vanguardia* (6 Nov. 1891); *La Renaixensa* (12 Nov. 1891); *L'Avenç* (30 Nov. 1891), 335; *La Veu de Catalunya* (6 Dec. 1891); *Ilustración Artística* (1892), no. 531, see Maragall, *Història de la Sala Parés*, ill. 45; *Chicago Daily Tribune* (14 June 1893); Raddin Scrapbook, vol. 2, Northwestern University, 1893, 114 (unidentified review); *Pèl & Ploma* (28 Oct. 1899), 3, no. 7; *La Vanguardia* (31 Oct. 1899); *La Veu de Catalunya* (31 Oct. 1899); *La Veu de Catalunya* (7 June 1900); Jordà, *Ramón Casas, pintor*, 23; Utrillo, "Història anecdòtica del Cau Ferrat," 36; Pla, *Santiago Rusiñol y su tiempo*, 110; Barcelona, *Exposición Ramón Casas*, 1958, 18; McCully, "Els Quatre Gats," 1975, 35–36, 153.

Exhibitions: Salon de Champ de Mars, Paris, 1891; Sala Parés, Barcelona, 1891; World's Columbian Exposition, Chicago, 1893, *Official Catalogue of Exhibits, pt. 10, Fine Arts, Spain*, no. 51, and *Revised Catalogue, Department of Fine Arts*, no. 139; Sala Parés, Barcelona, 1899; Sala Parés, Barcelona, 1900.

16 Ramón Casas.
Portrait of Erik Satie,
charcoal on paper, ca. 1891.
Private collection

9   *Anxiety*
   Ansiedad

The subject of interiors was not altogether new to nineteenth-century Spanish painting, for there had been a revival of interest in Dutch interiors, particularly genre scenes of the seventeenth century. What was novel in *modernista* interiors was the influence of French art. In some paintings, the "realism" of Manet, Degas, and contemporary photography is apparent in theme, point of view, and technique; while in other works, particularly those of Casas, there is a suggestion of "symbolist" intimacy. Hence, such moods as boredom, loneliness, melancholy, or even variations of consciousness such as sleep or drug-induced states, are suggested by the content and pictorial expression of these various interiors.

In *Anxiety* Casas selected a compact and highly evocative interior scene to communicate the mood of the title. A woman in white is sitting upright, leaning forward and looking beyond the room through partially opened double doors. (*Pentimenti* reveal that Casas originally oriented the woman seated in a rocking chair to face in the opposite direction.) The siphon bottle on the table next to the woman, given a bright touch of red paint, may relate to the illness of an unseen person in the room beyond. An amber light glows through the glass panes of the left-hand door and the object glimpsed in the opening appears to be a bed. However, there is no real narrative, no direct indication of content other than that given by the title. Rather, there is the suggestion of an unexplained presence in this quiet, intimate scene. The glowing light, the darkened interior, the partially opened doors, and the concerned attitude of the woman suggest a Maeterlinck-inspired theme: the unknown, the unexpected, both for the woman and for us, the spectators. Perhaps this mysterious presence is imminent death, for death, as in *L'Intruse*,[1] may pass by unnoticed visually, although its presence may be perceived on a different level.

1 *L'Intruse* was the first of Maeterlinck's plays to be performed publicly, when a benefit performance for Verlaine and Gauguin was given at Paul Fort's Théâtre d'Art in Paris on 21 May 1891. Two years later the play was performed in Catalan translation (as *L'intrusa*) at the second Festa Modernista in Sitges. In that production the *modernista* art critic Raimon Casellas took the leading role of the old, blind grandfather, and Rusiñol played the father.

Instituto Amatller, Barcelona

Ca. 1891; signed lower right: *R. Casas*. Oil on canvas; 58 x 47.5 cm.

Bibliography: McCully, "Els Quatre Gats," 1975, 238–41.

Exhibition: Sala Parés, Barcelona, 1900(?).

IO *Ramón Casas and Pere Romeu on a Tandem Bicycle*
Ramón Casas y Pere Romeu en un tandem

Casas's large painting, *Ramón Casas and Pere Romeu on a Tandem Bicycle*, was made specifically for the interior decoration of Els Quatre Gats in 1897 (see fig. 2). Although painted on canvas, the composition has the quality of a huge poster in its bold drawing and simplified forms. The original inscription boasted that "to ride a bicycle, you can't go with your back straight." The message described the attitude of the café founders, two of whom, Romeu and Casas, ride the tandem: that is, in order to make progress, you cannot worry about propriety; you break with tradition as was done at Els Quatre Gats. In 1900 this canvas was replaced in the *sala gran* by a second large composition by Casas (see Opisso's drawing, fig. 7), in which the tandem bicycle has given way to a car, symbolizing the new century.

Museo de Arte Moderno, Barcelona

1897; originally inscribed and signed upper right: *Per anar am bicicleta / No 's pot du l'esquena dreta / R. Casas.* Oil on canvas; 129 x 215 cm (cut down, cf. fig. 3).

Provenance: Els Quatre Gats; Plandiura Collection; Establecimientos Maragall, S.A.

Bibliography: *Pèl & Ploma*, no. 78 (July 1901), 62 (as *Fin de sigle XIX*); Jordà, "Ramón Casas," 1932, 108–9; Ráfols, *Ramón Casas, dibujante*, ill. 50; Barcelona, *Exposición Ramón Casas*, 24; Camon Aznar, José, "El modernismo en el Casón," *Goya*, no. 93 (Nov.–Dec. 1969), 135; McCully, "Els Quatre Gats," 1975, 180.

Exhibition: Casón del Buen Retiro, Madrid, 1969, *El modernismo en España*, no. 1-7.

II Poster: *Anis del Mono*

This rare printer's proof is a preliminary state of the poster design that won first prize in the Sala Parés competition of 1898, sponsored by the wealthy industrialist Vicente Bosch from nearby Badalona. Bosch wished to advertise his company's brand-name "Monkey" anise, Anis del Mono, with the winning posters. Casas actually submitted four designs to the competition, and the three that depicted a Spanish *chula*, wearing an embroidered shawl, were awarded prizes.[1] In this version and another, where the words *Anis del Mono* are embroidered on the woman's shawl, her glass of anise is filled by the monkey. Both posters were frequently reprinted and distributed in Barcelona, and also in Paris by Edmond Sagot. The third prize-winning design (fig. 17) is a variation on the first-prize poster and shows the monkey without his bottle of anise; there is also a change in the position of the lettering: *Anis del Mono* appears below and *Vicente Bosch* above the image.

1 According to Casellas ("Concurso de carteles en el Salon Parés," 4), the fourth poster depicted a woman seated at a table near the sea, lifting the veil of her hat to drink her liqueur.

Private collection

1898; signed in stone lower left: *R. Casas.*
Lithograph (preliminary state); 213.2 x 109.5 cm.

Bibliography (of final state): Casellas, Raimon, "Concurso de carteles en el Salón Parés," *La Vanguardia* (1 April 1898), 4; Deschamps, "L'Affiche espagnole," 421; "El cartel en Barcelona," *La Vanguardia* (15 July 1899), 4–5; Pica, Vittorio, *Attraverso gli Albi e le Cartelle*, Bergamo, 1902, 349; Utrillo, "L'obra d'en Casas," 325; Jordà, *Ramón Casas, pintor*, 42–43; Santos Torroella, *El cartel*, 23; Ráfols, *Ramón Casas, pintor*, 33; Schardt, Hermann, *Paris 1900*, New York, 1970, 46; Barnicoat, John, *A Concise History of Posters*, London, 1972, 27.

Exhibitions (of final state): Sala Parés, Barcelona, 1898; Palacio de la Virreina, Barcelona, 1958, *Exposición Ramón Casas*, no. 137, 38.

17 Ramón Casas.
Poster: *Anis del Mono*, 1898.
Private collection

I2 Poster: *Puchinel-lis: 4 Gats*

A second puppet theater, *putxinel-lis* (*puchinel-lis*), was added as a Quatre Gats attraction in late 1898. The new feature, primarily aimed towards a youthful audience, was publicized by this striking poster by Casas. In the role of "Punch" is Pere Romeu (cf. Romeu's head in the emblem Casas designed for Els Quatre Gats, as in the ceramic tiles shown in fig. 3), while the other puppet has a Pierrot-like face with large dark eyes. The poster, printed in red, yellow, black, and white, is a strong, rather bold composition. A drawing based upon the poster was used to advertise the *putxinel-lis* in the various periodicals that included notices of the event, such as *Quatre Gats* and *Pèl & Ploma*.

The puppeteer at Els Quatre Gats was the most celebrated *titellair* in Catalonia, Julio Pi. Pi came to Els Quatre Gats at the height of his career to manage the puppet theater. He had begun as a youth of about fifteen with a local puppeteer named Joaquim Sa'ez, whose theater was located in a café on the Carrer del Carme in Barcelona. From there Pi moved to a suburb of the city, Sabadell, in 1872, when he set up his own puppet show in a café on the Carrer de Migdia. There he gained an enormously popular reputation and developed a repertory of more than a hundred different plays.[1] He used a colloquial Catalan and his puppets were legendary, beloved characters among several generations of young people who came to know them. A cover of *Pèl & Ploma* (10 February 1900) by José-Luis Pellicer depicts a typical audience attending Pi's *putxinel-lis* theater at Els Quatre Gats.

1 Unfortunately, the archive that preserved these many works burned in Sabadell in 1887. Pi, however, with the help of his son Julià, continued presenting the majority of the works from memory. Pi was said to have prided himself in the selection of his characters and moods to fit a particular audience.

Museo de Arte Escénico, Barcelona

1898.
Lithograph; 53 x 38 cm.

Bibliography: *Quatre Gats*, nos. 1–10 (1899), 4; Pylax, "New Posters," 25; Deschamps, "L'Affiche espagnole," 422; *Pèl & Ploma*, nos. 1–20, 22, 23, 25, 27–30 (1899), nos. 32–34, 38–41, 46–52 (1900); Utrillo, "L'obra d'en Casas," 325; Bas i Gich, "Els Quatre Gats," 6; Jordà, *Ramón Casas, pintor*, 45; Ráfols, *Modernismo y modernistas*, 131; Ráfols, *Ramón Casas, dibujante*, 23, 33; Cirici, *El arte modernista catalán*, 345; Barcelona, *Quatre Gats, Primer Salón "Revista,"* 27; McCully, "El poster y Els Quatre Gats," 70, 72; McCully, "Els Quatre Gats," 1975, 195, ill. 28.

Exhibition: Palacio de la Virreina, Barcelona, 1958, *Exposición Ramón Casas*, no. 149.

13 Poster: *4 Gats: Pere Romeu*

Casas's poster for Els Quatre Gats depicts its proprietor Romeu seated at the bar of the establishment. Between him and the characteristic arch of the interior is a crowd of customers with their beer mugs raised high. The simplified figure of Romeu smoking a pipe, in his long coat and flat-brimmed hat, occupies almost half of the drawing and contrasts with the background where a sense of activity is gained through the sketchy use of the lithographer's crayon.

The lettering above Romeu, *4 Gats*, forms part of an inner frame that Casas incorporates in the design. The words *Pere Romeu* are cut out of the lower section, echoing the color of the background above. Below the inner frame on another version of the poster were the additional words: *Montesion—Barcelona, Se serveix beurer y menjar a totes hores*, proclaiming that food and drink were served at all hours.[1]

An earlier state of the poster, without any lettering, was also used as publicity for Els Quatre Gats in the form of postcards and small handouts, and was frequently reproduced in magazines. In addition, a preliminary design for the poster, which lacks not only the lettering but also the beer mugs on the bar counter, was printed for advertisements (fig. 18).

Little biographical information about Pere Romeu (ca. 1862–1908) is available to indicate just what his activities were prior to his contact with Miguel Utrillo in Montmartre in the early 1890s. Born in the small Catalan town of Torredembara (south of Barcelona, near the coast), Romeu went to Paris with an interest in art in the mid-1880s. In the cabaret milieu of Montmartre, he was attracted to Salis's café Le Chat Noir, to the shadow puppet theater, and to the colorful personality of Aristide Bruant, proprietor of Le Mirliton. Romeu was to base his style as *cabaretier* at Els Quatre Gats on the legendary Bruant, who was immortalized by Toulouse-Lautrec in many posters and drawings.

After his trip to Chicago in 1893 as a member of Marôt's theater Les Ombres Parisiennes, Romeu returned to Catalonia, where he participated in the *modernista* festivals in Sitges and then ran Els Quatre Gats from 1897 to its closing in 1903. After that date Romeu remained in Barcelona and tried a new business venture, the Sportsmen's Club, a roller-skating rink. After only one year he closed the club and worked in the car business, automobiles being an enthusiasm he shared with Casas. In Rusiñol's opinion, this work held no real professional attraction for the colorful personality who had dreamed of "castles in the sky." When Romeu died in December 1908, aged less than fifty, Rusiñol wrote that Romeu "was accustomed to drinking the happy wine of the inn and had to turn to gas at the garage—and it killed him!"[2]

1 See McCully, "El poster y Els Quatre Gats," 71.
2 Rusiñol, "En Pere Romeu," *Obres completes*, 769.

Museo de Arte Moderno, Barcelona

1900; signed in stone lower right: *R. Casas.*
Lithograph; 58 x 38.5 cm.

Bibliography: *Pèl & Ploma*, nos. 35–36 (Jan.-Feb. 1900); *La Publicidad* (4 April 1900), 2; *Joventut* (12 April 1900), 144; *Pluma y Lapiz* (1901), 704; Jordà, *Ramón Casas, pintor*, 41–45; Jordà, "Ramón Casas," 1932, 108–9; Ráfols, *Modernismo y modernistas*, ill. 45; Ráfols, "Los carteles '1900,'" 35–36; Ráfols, *Ramón Casas, dibujante*, 33; Santos Torroella, *El cartel*, 25; Bas i Gich, "Els Quatre Gats," 7; McCully, "El poster y Els Quatre Gats," 71, 73; Camon Aznar, José, "El modernismo en el Casón," *Goya*, no. 93 (Nov.-Dec. 1969), 138; McCully, "Els Quatre Gats," 1975, ill. 30.

Exhibitions: Palacio de la Virreina, Barcelona, 1958, *Exposición Ramón Casas*, no. 150; Casón del Buen Retiro, Madrid, 1969, *El modernismo en España*, no. v-3.

18 Ramón Casas.
Printed advertisement:
4 Gats: Pere Romeu, ca. 1900.
Private collection

I4 Poster: *Sífilis*

Casas's poster is an advertisement for a sanatorium for syphilitics, which claims to offer an "absolute and radical cure." While similar advertisements of cures for drug addiction and venereal disease can be found in periodicals and newspapers from the turn of the century, they are much less often seen in the form of posters. In those days, before the discovery of penicillin, the cure referred to here was probably the use of mercury and potassium iodide, the most prevalent means of treating the disease before 1910, when a less dangerous and more effective compound of arsenic was developed. The existence of sanatoriums is explained by the fact that the process involved a prolonged period of time, as we are told in the 1911 *Encyclopaedia Britannica*: "An English physician said 'Syphilis once, syphilis ever.' This is not true. If the individual places himself unreservedly and continually under the treatment of a trustworthy practitioner, he may confidently look forward to a cure. . . . Syphilis is a disease which peculiarly calls for treatment, and that treatment, to be effectual, must be prolonged."

In the poster the message is conveyed by means of a fatal temptress, who entices the viewer with a white lily while concealing a black and green snake behind her back. Wrapped in a deep magenta, black-fringed shawl, she is alluringly turned away from the viewer who, though knowing her secret, is still taken in or attracted. She is the same dark-haired Spanish *maja* or *chula* type of woman to be found in Casas's more famous posters of 1898 for Anis del Mono [11], although here the artist has added a greater air of mystery, transforming her into a *femme fatale*. The unusual and jarring color scheme—a dark green border and the magenta-clothed woman against a deep ochre background—further contributes to the mood of the picture.

In contrast to the relatively flat, more poster-like style of the *Anis del Mono* designs, Casas has here achieved a sketchy quality by using the lithographer's crayon to obtain the effect of drawing on rough paper. This sketchiness is heightened by the visible reworking of the woman's left hand and the lily. In style and format the poster is similar to Casas's poster for *Pèl & Ploma*,[1] which was printed by the same firm, J. Thomas, in Barcelona. An earlier state of the *Sífilis* poster also appeared as a cover of *Pèl & Ploma*, no. 58 (15 August 1900). P.C.

1 Reproduced in Madrid, *El modernismo en Espanã*, no. V-5.

Private collection

1900; signed in stone lower left: *R. Casas*; printer's notation: *J. Thomas, Barcelona.*
Lithograph; 71.5 x 34.5 cm.

I5 *Devil*

Three illustrations by Casas accompanied a humorous vignette entitled "Sin sesos," by Juan Buscón, in the first issue of the periodical *Hispania*. The story concerns an excursion up to the heavens by the devil and his dispute with a somewhat stuffy Eternal Father about God's purpose in creating a new model of human being, one without any brains.

The first and most striking of the three illustrations is the *Devil*, shown posing with his wings spread "like a gigantic and infernal butterfly," after having shined his horns, talons, and tail for the trip. Casas applies his characteristic drawing style to good dramatic effect: heavy black patches of ink are combined with brusquely stylized lines to convey the devil's haughtily menacing character. The slightly distracting effect of the white corrections in the original would be eliminated once the drawing was reproduced by a photographic process.   E.A.

Private collection

1899; inscribed on verso: *Sin Sesos por Juan Buscón.*
Drawing for publication, ink with white watercolor corrections on heavy drawing paper; 25.5 x 18.5 cm.

Provenance: Establecimientos Maragall, S.A., Barcelona.

Bibliography: *Hispania*, no. 1 (1899), 12.

Exhibition: Sala Parés, Barcelona, 1968, *100 Dibujos originales para la revista Hispania*, no. 3.

16 *Girl in Street Costume*

Casas contributed drawings for advertisements to many Spanish magazines at the turn of the century. His favorite model was a fashionably dressed young woman, such as the figure in *Girl in Street Costume*. Note that the woman's right hand has been altered; its original position, holding a liqueur glass, is now covered by the blue chalk of the background. The earlier version suggests that this drawing may have originally been intended as a design for an advertisement. A closely related drawing (on the back cover of *Pèl & Ploma*, no. 98, October 1902) uses the same model, standing and similarly dressed, to advertise the Madrid publishing house, B. Rodriguez Serra.

The present drawing is inscribed to Charles Deering (1852–1927), a Chicago businessman, amateur painter, and art collector who formed a close friendship with Casas during the early part of this century.[1] Deering himself studied painting for a brief period in 1893 in the Paris studio of the Swedish artist Anders Zorn. He was also friendly with a number of artists in Paris, including John Singer Sargent. After returning to the family business in Chicago, however, Deering subsequently confined his interest in art to collecting.

Deering was particularly fond of Spain and established part-time residence first in Sitges in the old hospital, which he had remodeled and called Mar-i-Cel, located next to the Cau Ferrat. There he housed his growing collection of both contemporary and older Spanish art. In 1908 he invited Casas to accompany him to the United States for a one-year stay. During that visit Casas was commissioned as a portrait painter by family friends of Deering in several American cities. In 1916 Deering moved his collection and his Spanish residence to the castle at Tamarit, where he also set up a studio for Casas. The majority of Deering's collection of Spanish art is now located in the United States, in both public (principally the Art Institute of Chicago) and private collections.

1 Deering first noticed Casas's *Portrait of Erik Satie* [8] at the World's Columbian Exposition in 1893, and later met the artist in Paris, where he asked Casas to paint a portrait of his daughter. Numerous drawings of the many excursions and shared experiences of the two friends, particularly from the years 1908 to 1910, record the warm nature of their friendship. Several of these drawings are in the Museo de Arte Moderno in Barcelona (nos. 23632–39) and many others are still in the collections of Deering's descendants.

Art Institute of Chicago, Charles Deering Collection (1927.2458)

Ca. 1902; inscribed and signed lower right: *To my friend Deering, R. Casas* (superimposed over pencil signature: *R. Casas*).
Blue, black, and orange chalks on paper; 63.5 x 27.8 cm.

Provenance: Charles Deering; gift of Mrs. Chauncy McCormick and Mrs. Richard E. Danielson in 1927.

To my friend Deering
R. Casas

17 *Girl at the Piano*

This drawing was used in an advertisement for a piano store, which appeared frequently on the inside cover of *Pèl & Ploma* with the words: *Vda. de P. Estella (Antigua casa Bernareggi), Pianos, Gran Via—275—Barcelona*. The drawing was reproduced in white on colored paper and was slightly cropped on either side in the final advertisement. The seal of the magazine appears at the lower right. On special occasions, original Casas drawings for *Pèl & Ploma* were given to subscribers and friends of the journal as gifts; *Girl at the Piano* was probably such a gift from Casas to Charles Deering.

Art Institute of Chicago, Charles Deering Collection (1927.2460)

Ca. 1902; signed lower left: *R. Casas*; embossed lower right: *Pèl & Ploma*. Charcoal, pastel, and pencil on paper; 32.5 x 25 cm.

Provenance: Charles Deering; gift of Mrs. Chauncy McCormick and Mrs. Richard E. Danielson in 1927.

Adrià Gual Queralt
1872–1944

Adrià Gual first studied painting and drawing at La Llotja and in the studio of Pedro Borrell. In 1893 he joined Nonell, Vallmitjana, Canals, and Mir in their group, the Colla de Sant Martí. During the 1890s Gual also worked in his father's lithographic atelier and gained success as a poster designer, winning recognition in the 1898 poster exhibition sponsored by the Ayuntamiento de Barcelona. Gual is perhaps best remembered as an enthusiast for modern theater, which he promoted at his own symbolist-inspired Teatre Intim, founded by him in Barcelona in 1898. He continued to write plays and prose, and to direct and teach theater in the Catalan capital until his death in 1944.

18 Poster: *Llibre d'horas*

Gual's book, *Llibre d'horas* ("Book of Hours"), was advertised by this poster, which Gual designed and produced in his father's lithographic atelier in 1899. Like much *modernista* decorative art, it is stylistically eclectic and combines curvilinear art-nouveau forms, symbolist coloration, and calligraphy based on traditional Spanish models. Iconographically it resembles Miguel Utrillo's 1897 poster announcing the publication of Santiago Rusiñol's *Oracions*.[1] Gual's poster, however, is graphically less bold; through its evocative coloration, energetic plant forms, and convincing but slightly unnatural space, the poster conveys a mood appropriate to Gual's own literary symbolism.   M.F.

1 Reproduced in Madrid, *El modernismo en España*, no. V-20.

Private collection

1899; printed monogram upper left incorporating the artist's initials *AGQ* and the year *1899*; printer's notation: *Tirat a Ca'n Gual*. Lithograph; 52.5 x 42.8 cm.

Provenance: Colnaghi & Co., Ltd., 1973.

Bibliography: Deschamps, "L'Affiche espagnole," 423; Cirici, *El arte modernista catalán*, 212.

Exhibitions: Casón del Buen Retiro, Madrid, 1969, *El modernismo en España*, no. V-7; Colnaghi & Co., Ltd., London, 1973, *Prints from Spain, Portugal and Latin America*, no. 75; Sala Parés, Barcelona, 1974.

Isidro Nonell Monturiol
1873–1911

Nonell's earliest artistic training included study in the studios of Mirabent, Martinez Altes, and Graner, and at the art academy La Llotja. Works by Nonell were included in group shows in Barcelona beginning in 1893; his drawings appeared frequently in Barcelona periodicals, such as *La Vanguardia*, after 1894. Nonell's association with Canals and the Colla de Sant Martí led to an early preference for themes dealing with marginal groups, particularly gypsies and cretins. Nine works by Nonell were included in the first exhibition at Els Quatre Gats in 1897, and in December of 1898 he had a one-man show there. In Paris, he exhibited in the "Quinzième Exposition des Peintres Impressionistes et Symbolistes" at Le Barc de Boutteville in 1898, and at Vollard's in 1899. From the turn of the century until his death in 1911, Nonell frequently exhibited in Barcelona and at the Salon des Indépendants in Paris; in 1903 he exhibited at the Libre Esthétique in Brussels.

19 *Annunciation in the Slums*
L'anunciata

This drawing, published in a special New Year's Day issue of *La Vanguardia* in 1897, shows the developing awareness among some of the Quatre Gats group of the power of social statement in art. An angel dressed in white displays a scroll with the inscription *Gloria in excelsis Deo* to a group of pathetic individuals in an industrial slum. Nonell portrays the old, the demented, and the ill together, in the face of possible salvation, as hopeless and disbelieving. Drawings of similar subjects by Nonell, Canals, Opisso, and Luis Graner, among others, appeared frequently in Barcelona periodicals throughout the 1890s. One member of the Quatre Gats group who was impressed with Nonell and the subject of the poor was Picasso. In his *End of the Road* (fig. 15) of 1899, the poor and needy proceed on foot or are carried up the hillside to a cemetery; the rich ride in chariots on a higher road only to meet the same fate, the angel of death.

Museo de Arte Moderno, Barcelona

Ca. 1892; signed lower right: *Nonell*. Conté crayon and charcoal on paper; 32 x 35.5 cm.

Provenance: Raimon Casellas.

Bibliography: *La Vanguardia* (1 Jan. 1897); Jardí, *Nonell*, 289, ill. 208; Cervera, *Modernismo*, ill. 40.

Isidro Nonell

20 *Misery*
La miseria; Dues gitanes

Misery, a dark composition portraying two gypsy women, is representative of the work done by Nonell after the 1890s in both subject matter and technique. The theme of gypsies, which dominates Nonell's production from 1901 to his death in 1911, is an outgrowth of a basically *modernista* concern. The gypsy, contrasting with the modern woman favored by artists such as Casas, stood for a way of life that lay apart from the mainstream, along the margins of a developing urban society. For Nonell, the gypsy woman represented the passion of life itself. It is in this fundamental attitude toward the human struggle, as symbolized by the poor and alienated, that Nonell influenced Picasso in his own choice of figures on the margins of society, particularly in the years 1902 to 1904, to express his personal concern with the human condition.

In technique, the concentration on one- or two-figure compositions, such as *Misery*, complements Nonell's determined investigation into the formal possibilities of his medium, oil on canvas. Under the influence of French painting, particularly the work of Cézanne, Nonell stylistically breaks away from his contemporaries in Barcelona and develops an approach based on a thick, somewhat abbreviated brush stroke, which through contrast of color and direction builds form and enriches the surface of the canvas. The coexistence of a comparable formal development in the work of Picasso, stimulated in part by Nonell in Barcelona and then continued in Paris, in turn contributed to Nonell's own investigations.

Museo de Arte Moderno, Barcelona

1904; signed lower left: *Nonell, 1904*; signed and dated on verso: *Nonell, 1904.*
Oil on canvas; 75 x 100 cm.

Provenance: Francisco Labarta; acquired in 1922.

Bibliography: *Catálogo del Museo de Bellas Artes*, Barcelona, 1924, no. 3, 155; *Art*, vol. 1, no. 10 (July 1934), 340, ill. 127; Merli, Joan, *Isidro Nonell*, Barcelona, 1938, ill. 11; Barcelona, *Guía del Museo de Arte Moderno*, 41; Nonell, *Isidro Nonell: su vida y su obra*, 210, pl. 73; Larco, *La pintura española moderna y contemporánea*, vol. 2, 11 (as *Mujeres dolorosas*); Gaya Nuño, *La pintura española del siglo XX*, 33; Garrut, *Dos siglos de pintura catalana (XIX–XX)*, 228–29.

Exhibitions: Barcelona, 1918, *Exposició d'Art* (label on back of frame, no. 55); Madrid, 1951, *Precursores y maestros de la pintura española contemporánea*, 84; Barcelona, 1955, *Precursores y maestros del arte contemporáneo*, 12; Palacio de la Virreina, Barcelona, 1962, *Exposición Isidro Nonell*, no. 18; Madrid, 1966, "Exposición Nacional de Bellas Artes."

Isidro Nonell

21 *Seated Figures*

The drawing represents four figures, three women and a man, sitting on a bench; the women seem to be dozing, the man is smoking a pipe. Seated or crouching female figures, their faces averted from the spectator as if absorbed in some inner thought, became Nonell's almost unique thematic preoccupation after the turn of the century. Such figures were usually gypsies or beggars and seem to be a development of his previous concern for the poor and those disinherited by life. The painter's preference for such themes was first expressed with the series of drawings of popular types from Barcelona that he contributed to the newspaper *La Vanguardia* in 1894, and followed two years later with the famous series of caricatures of the cretins at Caldes de Bohí. The present work is, both in subject matter and style, close to a drawing by Nonell of a woman sitting on a stone bench, also dating to 1909, at the Museo de Arte Moderno in Barcelona.[1] However, *Seated Figures* contains neither the biting irony nor the bitter social criticism of most of Nonell's similar works. On the contrary, the mood suggested is one of tranquillity and bliss in the enjoyment of the sun and the open air. The light pastel shades of the watercolor wash also reinforce the overall tone of optimism.   N.M.A.

1 See Jardí, *Nonell*, ill. 153.

Private collection

1909; initialed and dated lower right: *n 09*.
Conté crayon and watercolor on paper; 15 x 10 cm.

Provenance: Establecimientos Maragall, S.A., Barcelona.

Exhibition: Sala Parés, Barcelona, 1969, *Isidre Nonell, 33 dibuixos exposats a la Sala Parés*, no. 21.

Ricardo Opisso Sala
1880–1966

Ricardo Opisso, a self-taught draftsman from Tarragona, was introduced to the Quatre Gats group by the painter Joaquim Mir, whom Opisso had met while working as an assistant to the architect Gaudí on the Sagrada Familia church in Barcelona. Opisso's many drawings of the various individuals who gathered at Els Quatre Gats have since served as an important record of those years and of life at the café (see fig. 7). Opisso worked primarily as an illustrator and his drawings appeared in a variety of Barcelona periodicals, including *Luz*, *Quatre Gats*, *Hispania*, and *La Vanguardia*, among many others. In 1902 he made his first trip to Paris and thereafter occasionally contributed illustrations to French periodicals, such as *Le Rire* and *Frou-Frou*.

22 *Man with a Pack*

23 *Peasants*

Both *Man with a Pack* and *Peasants* reflect Opisso's continuing concern with the subject of the working class and the routines of everyday life. Opisso shared this interest with others from the Quatre Gats group, such as Nonell, Canals, and Picasso. The inner frame drawing in *Peasants*, delineating the landscape setting, suggests that the sketch was probably a preliminary idea for a magazine illustration.

Private collection

Ca. 1905; signed lower right: *Opisso*. Pencil on paper; (22) 21.7 x 18 cm; (23) 20.5 x 25.5 cm.

Pablo Ruíz Picasso
1881–1973

Picasso's association with Els Quatre Gats probably began in late 1898, although he had already met some of the younger group, such as Manuel Pallarés, in 1895 when Picasso's family moved to Barcelona. Picasso also briefly attended classes at La Llotja in 1895 and won an honorable mention for the painting *Science and Charity* (Museo Picasso, Barcelona), which he sent to the 1897 Exposición Nacional in Madrid. His first Barcelona exhibition was held in the *sala gran* of Els Quatre Gats in 1900. The following year Utrillo and Casas, as editors of *Pèl & Ploma*, sponsored a show of Picasso's pastels at the Sala Parés. During the Quatre Gats years, Picasso's drawings were published in various Barcelona periodicals, including *Pèl & Ploma, Joventut, Catalunya Artística*, and *El Liberal*. Evidence of the extraordinary importance of those years for Picasso can be found in both his work and his stylistic development. In tribute to them, he made a donation in 1970 of some two thousand drawings and paintings to the Picasso Museum in Barcelona, established by his lifelong friend Jaime Sabartés, whom he had first met at Els Quatre Gats.

24 *Portrait of Josef Cardona*

Picasso's friendship with the sculptor Josep Cardona i Furró (1878–1923) probably began in 1897, when Cardona was a student at the Barcelona academy La Llotja. Cardona (brother of Santiago Cardona, the painter) was the son of a corset-maker who had a shop, called El Perfil, on Escudillers Blancs, no. 1, in Barcelona. Cardona's studio in the same building was a gathering place for many artists and poets in the late 1890s. Picasso rented a small studio in the building and worked there regularly in 1899, and his portrait of Cardona (one of three known portraits of the sculptor by Picasso)[1] was done during this period. Palau Fabre has suggested that the drawings Picasso made of his friends who met at Cardona's studio were probably shown in Picasso's 1900 exhibition at Els Quatre Gats.[2] Note that Picasso's dedication is in Catalan; it is quite likely that the majority of the group with whom he associated in Barcelona spoke and wrote Catalan, which he had learned by this date.

1 See also Z.VI.264 and Z.XXI.115.
2 Palau Fabre, *Picasso i els seus amics catalans*, 55.

Private collection

1899; inscribed and signed center left: *Al volgut amich Cardona—P. Ruíz Picasso.*
Conté crayon on paper; 38 x 30.4 cm.

Provenance: Galerie Pierre, Paris; acquired in 1934 by Dr. McKinley Helm; acquired in 1957.

Bibliography: Z.XXI.121; Daix D.I.5; Palau Fabre, *Picasso i els seus amics catalans*, 55.

Exhibitions: Fogg Art Museum, Cambridge, Mass., 1934; Santa Barbara Museum of Art, 1961, "School of Paris"; University of California at Los Angeles, 1961, *"Bonne Fête" Monsieur Picasso*, no. 48; Phoenix Art Museum, 1962, "Paintings, Sculpture & Drawings from the Collections of Margaret Mallory and Ala Story"; Art Gallery of Toronto, 1964, *Picasso and Man*, no. 2; Santa Barbara Museum of Art and the San Francisco Palace of the Legion of Honor, 1966, "Two Collections"; Santa Barbara Museum of Art, 1976.

Pablo Picasso

25 *Portrait of Evelí Torent*

Picasso's portrait of the painter Evelí Torent Marsans (1876–1940) is one of two known portraits of his friend from Els Quatre Gats.[1] Prior to Torent's association with the Quatre Gats group, he studied briefly with Martí Alsina and had his first exhibition of paintings in Barcelona in 1896. In the following year, two canvases by Torent were included in the inaugural exhibition of Els Quatre Gats, and in 1899 he was featured in a one-man show in the *sala gran* of the café. In addition, Torent contributed to local *modernista* publications, including *Luz*, *Quatre Gats*, and *Pèl & Ploma*. In 1901 Torent moved to Paris where, like Picasso, he was represented by Pere Manyac, and achieved success as a portrait painter (later commissions included portraits of King George V and President Woodrow Wilson).

1 See also Z.XXI.117.

Detroit Institute of Arts, Founders Society Purchase, D. M. Ferry, Jr. Fund (38.34)

1899; inscribed and signed lower left: *A mi amigo E Torent, P. Ruíz Picasso.* Charcoal on cream, laid paper; 48.8 x 32.3 cm.

Provenance: Mrs. Cornelius J. Sullivan; acquired in 1938.

Bibliography: Z.XXI.118; Daix D.I.4; Lesley, Parker, *Detroit Institute of Arts Bulletin*, vol. 18, no. 7 (April 1939), 3, ill. 6; Palau Fabre, *Picasso i els seus amics catalans*, 94.

Exhibition: Art Gallery of Toronto, 1964, *Picasso and Man*, no. 3.

Pablo Picasso

26 *Leaving the Exposition Universelle*
La Sortie de l'exposition

In this previously unpublished drawing made in Paris at the time of the 1900 Exposition Universelle and Picasso's first visit to France, the young artist depicts himself in the company of two women and several of his Barcelona friends. From left to right are an unidentified woman, Picasso, Ramón Pichot, Miguel Utrillo, Carles Casagemas, and a second woman who may be Germaine, with whom Casagemas fell in love on this visit to Paris. The merrymakers are linked together arm in arm leaving the exhibition buildings: Casagemas is still carrying a wine glass; Utrillo is kicking up his heels; and Picasso seems to be supported by his woman companion and the rather serious Pichot. A much smaller but closely related drawing by Picasso includes Ramón Casas between Pichot and Casagemas.[1] Casas himself published a drawing in 1900 of a female ticket-seller in front of the same Exposition structure as in the Picasso drawings (*Pèl & Ploma*, 15 August 1900, 10).

Picasso's extraordinary use of charcoal with touches of color is particularly noteworthy in this unusually large drawing. Quick, deliberate lines of varying thickness and direction shape the animated movement of the overall composition and differentiate the individual personalities in the group.

1 Palau Fabre, "1900: A Friend of His Youth," 8.

Acquavella Galleries, Inc., New York

1900; signed lower right: *P. Ruíz Picasso*.
Charcoal, colored chalks, and pencil on paper; 47.8 x 61 cm.

Provenance: Galerie Kate Perls, Paris; private collection, South Carolina.

27 *Picasso in Madrid with Four Friends*

In this drawing Picasso groups several male figures in overcoats and mufflers on a hillside with cropped trees suggesting a wintry scene. Gathered together are an unknown male at the left, Cornuti, Asis de Soler, Picasso (with a cane), and the poet Lozano on the far right. A rich linear network unites them as a group against the barren, dark surroundings, while their faces are left the white of the paper.

This drawing was made in Madrid for publication in the art journal *Arte Joven*, which Picasso and his friend, the writer Francisco Asis de Soler, published jointly in Madrid in 1901. Their little magazine (of which only five issues appeared from March to June) was modeled on the Catalan journal *Pèl & Ploma*.[1] It seems that Picasso and Soler had hopes of implanting a brand of Catalan *modernismo* in Madrid, and *Arte Joven* was a first effort in that direction. In addition to articles and drawings by the young editors, there were invited contributions from the editors' Barcelona friends as well as from writers whom they met at Madrid's famed *tertulia*, the Café Madrid. The issue of 31 March 1901, for example, included articles by representatives of the literary "generation of '98," Pio Baroja and Miguel de Unamuno. Following the model of *Pèl & Ploma*, the publication often included portraits by Picasso or Ricardo Baroja of contributing writers and artists. In addition, reviews of new art journals, both in Spanish and in Catalan, and notices of exhibitions and concerts were regular features.

1 The editors of *Pèl & Ploma* (Utrillo and Casas) reviewed the first issue of *Arte Joven*, noting that Picasso was the real promoter of the venture and that the publication was off to a good start, especially with regard to his illustrations; see *Pèl & Ploma*, 15 March 1901, 7.

Private collection

1901; signed lower right: *P. Ruíz Picasso.*
Drawing for publication, crayon on paper; 24 x 31.7 cm.

Provenance: Louis Goldschmidt; Christie's, London, 1960; Mr. and Mrs. Irving Felt, New York; Knoedler, Paris; acquired in 1965.

Bibliography: Z.I.36; Daix D.III.5; *Arte Joven*, no. 2 (15 April 1901), 4; Sabartés, *Picasso: documents iconographiques*, ill. 67; Cirici, *Picasso avant Picasso*, ill. 34; Blunt and Pool, *Picasso*, ill. 53; Palau Fabre, *Picasso per Picasso*, 55.

Exhibitions: Knoedler, Paris, 1965, *Picasso*, no. 11; Morris Gallery, Toronto, 1972, *Toronto's Picassos*, no. 2; National Gallery of Canada, Ottawa, 1976–77, *European Drawings from Canadian Collections, 1500–1900*, no. 60.

Pablo Picasso

28 *At the Cabaret*

Many of Picasso's drawings of the interiors of cafés, cabarets, and other places of entertainment appear to be made directly from life. In *At the Cabaret* a rapidity of recording is suggested by the deliberate, repeated lines whose contrasted directions serve to distinguish form. A circular movement in the composition begins with the foreground figure seated at the left of the round table, continues in the standing woman, and follows the seated group around the table, ending with the almost faceless figure at the right.

Art Institute of Chicago, Lewis L. Coburn Memorial Collection (1933.527)

Ca. 1901; signed lower right: *Picasso*. Black, orange, and blue crayons on paper; 12.5 x 21.4 cm.

Bibliography: Z.xxi.174; Daix D.iv.1.

Exhibitions: Birmingham Museum of Art, Birmingham, Alabama, 1952; R. S. Johnson International Gallery, Chicago, 1973, *Homage to Picasso*, no. 1.

29 *Woman with Cape*

Woman with Cape, according to Picasso, is the portrait of a young French woman who modeled for another painting done in Paris in 1901, *Reclining Figure*.[1] Picasso's bust-length *Woman with Cape* also relates to the portraits of women he had painted in Madrid and Barcelona earlier in 1901. In the Spanish canvases Picasso experimented with color and an energized brush stroke, which reflect his admiration both for Spanish portrait artists such as Velázquez and Goya, and also for the French art he saw on his first Parisian visit in 1900, represented by artists such as Manet, Van Gogh, and the neo-impressionists. In *Woman with Cape*, brush stroke and color generate form and enliven the entire surface of the canvas.

1 Daix, 189; for the related *Reclining Figure*, see Daix v.52.

Cleveland Museum of Art, Bequest of Leonard C. Hanna, Jr. (58.44)

Ca. 1901; signed upper left: *Picasso*. Oil on canvas; 73 x 50 cm.

Provenance: John Quinn, New York; Libaude, Paris; Madame Demotte, Paris; Robert Lebel, Paris; Reinhardt Galleries, New York; Courvoisier Galleries, San Francisco; Leonard C. Hanna, Jr.

Bibliography: Z.VI.542; Daix v.76; Cleveland Museum of Art, *In Memoriam Leonard C. Hanna, Jr.*, 1958, ill. 27; Martin-Méry, Gilberte, "La Peinture française dans les collections américaines," *Plaisir de France* (May 1966), ill. 19 (as *La Femme au chapeau*); Henning, Edward B., "Bouteille, Verre, et Fourchette," *Cleveland Museum of Art Bulletin* (Sept. 1972), ill. 196.

Exhibitions: Galerie La Nouvelle Renaissance, Paris, 1929; Galerie Demotte, Paris, 1931, "Picasso," no. 2; Reinhardt Galleries, New York, 1936; Jacques Seligman & Co., New York, 1937, *Exhibition of 19th and 20th Century Paintings*, no. 1; Courvoisier Galleries, San Francisco, 1937, *French Paintings 19th and 20th Centuries*, no. 12; Knoedler, New York, 1947, *Picasso before 1907*, no. 10; Bordeaux, 1966, "La Peinture française dans les collections américaines," no. 109.

30 *Pere Romeu—4 Gats*

In this remarkable drawing Picasso portrays himself seated in the left fore-ground in the company of several of his friends in the interior of Els Quatre Gats; from left to right are Romeu, Rocarol, Fontbona, Angel F. de Soto (also called Patas), and Jaime Sabartés. Completing the composition is a dog at the lower right of the interior furnishings designed by Puig i Cada-falch. Picasso's rich network of cross-hatching and variations in the direc-tion and thickness of line, often emphasizing the grain of the paper, serve to individualize the various figures seated around the table.

The previously unpublished verso of the large sheet (fig. 19) reveals that Picasso first intended to show himself seen from the back, straddling a chair in front of a standing Romeu. In the completed design, he turns him-self around, showing a bearded face and holding a cane. His seated posi-tion two-dimensionally continues the figure of Romeu, who now sits be-hind him to the left of the table. The change gives Picasso a more im-portant place in the group.

In the final version, lighter pencil lines beneath the drawing indicate a few further changes; note that the position of the word *Carrer* has been changed. The message above, "Food and drink are served at all hours," and the words below, *Pere Romeu—4 Gats*, suggest that this drawing was used as an advertisement itself or was a poster design.

Private collection

1902; signed lower left with circled initial -P-; inscription above: *Es serveix Beure y Menjar a totes hores*; inscrip-tion below: *Pere Romeu—4 Gats, Carrer de Montesión*; verso: pencil drawing (see fig. 19).
India ink and pencil on paper; 31 x 34 cm.

Provenance: Plandiura Collection, Barcelona; Knoedler, Paris; acquired in 1965.

Bibliography: Z.VI.90; Daix IV.140; Cirici, *Picasso avant Picasso*, 43; Sabartés, *Picasso: documents icono-graphiques*, ill. 67; Horodisch, Abra-ham, *Pablo Picasso als Buchkunstler*, Frankfurt am Main, 1957, 2; Penrose, *Picasso*, 54; Daix, Pierre, *Picasso*, Paris, 1964, 21; Blunt and Pool, *Picasso*, 53; Palau Fabre, *Picasso en Cataluña*, ill. 71; McCully, "El poster y Els Quatre Gats," 73; Palau Fabre, *Picasso per Picasso*, 83; Lladó, "El Picasso de Els Quatre Gats," 10; Lecaldano, Paolo, *The Complete Paintings of Picasso*, London, 1971, 85; Elgar, Frank and Maillard, Robert, *Picasso*, New York, 1972, ill. 3; Porzio, Domenico and Valsecchi, Marco, *Picasso*, London, 1974, 242; McCully, "Els Quatre Gats," 1975, 201–2, ill. 30.

Exhibitions: Sala Parés, Barcelona, 1954, *Quatre Gats, Primer Salon "Revista,"* 1954, 19; Knoedler, Paris, 1965, *Picasso*, no. 14; Frankfurter Kunstverein, Frankfurt, 1965, *Exhibi-tion 150 Handzeichnungen aus sieben Jahrzehten*, no. 1; Morris Gallery, Toronto, 1972, *Toronto's Picassos*, no. 6.

19 Pablo Picasso. Pencil drawing on verso of *Pere Romeu—4 Gats* [30]. The standing figure is Romeu, the seated Picasso. Private collection

31 *Crouching Woman*
La Miséreuse accroupie

Picasso's *Crouching Woman* is representative of the principal thematic and painterly concerns of his so-called Blue Period, which find their origin in his Spanish experience. These years, from approximately 1901 to the end of 1903, correspond to a period of indecision on the part of the artist, who had broken with his family and would, in 1904, permanently leave his country. Works of the period, such as *Crouching Woman*, reveal a preoccupation with the dilemma of the individual whose position is economically or socially insecure; in this way they become personal statements for Picasso about aspects of his own life at the time.

Picasso shared an interest with his Quatre Gats friends, particularly Nonell, in the changing structure of Spanish society and its effects on the individual. With the move to the large city, those who would normally be cared for in the village, such as the ill, retarded, or poor, are cast aside. Their marginal position forces them to resort to life on the street as beggars, entertainers, or prostitutes. *Crouching Woman*, like Nonell's gypsies, is one of many similar figures Picasso painted that were inspired by this theme.

Picasso's Blue Period also coincides with a new concentration on certain formal problems, which allow for his own stylistic development. The limitation of the palette to darker tones, predominantly blue, not only conveys the solitary mood of his subjects but also focuses on the structure of the composition itself. In *Crouching Woman*, for example, the general shape of the figure is echoed in the dark area at the left, which may be a curtain or shadow. The lighter patch above the woman's right knee compositionally balances the light area and general shape of her face surrounded by a white scarf, while a simple horizontal mark at the lower right attaches the figure to the setting, giving her a sense of weight. The attention paid to the contained contour of the woman emphasizes her isolation, while providing a rhythm of shapes within the formal composition. The mood and attitude of this figure are comparable to Nonell's gypsies of the same period (cf. *Misery* [20], which was made two years later).[1] The building of form with a thick, repeated brush stroke, as in the area of the head and knees particularly, also suggests a similar painterly technique.

1 Blunt and Pool, for example, compare *Crouching Woman* formally to Nonell's *Group of the Poor* from the cretin series of 1896 (see *Picasso*, ills. 69, 70, 71, 72).

Art Gallery of Ontario, Toronto, anonymous gift (63/1)

1902; signed upper left: *Picasso*. Oil on canvas; 101.3 x 66 cm.

Provenance: Justin K. Thannhauser, Munich; Professor and Mrs. Bruno Mendel; acquired in 1963.

Bibliography: Z.I.121; Daix VII.5; Blunt and Pool, *Picasso*, ill. 71; Daix, Pierre, *Picasso*, Paris, 1964, 36; Lecaldano, Paolo, *The Complete Paintings of Picasso*, London, 1971, 89, ill. 25 (as *Crouching Beggar*); Cervera, *Modernismo*, ill. 43 (as *Mendicant*).

Exhibitions: Art Gallery of Toronto, 1964, *Picasso and Man*, no. 13; Vancouver Art Gallery, 1966, "Treasures from the Art Gallery of Toronto"; Art Gallery of Ontario, Toronto, 1975, *Puvis de Chavannes and the Modern Tradition*, no. 74.

32 *Drawings of Sebastià Junyer-Vidal and Other Figures*

Among the various figures included by Picasso in this sketch is his close friend from Els Quatre Gats, the painter Sebastià Junyer-Vidal, whose face appears twice in the upper right-hand portion of the sheet.[1] Picasso portrayed Junyer-Vidal more often than any other friend of the period in his drawings and paintings between 1901 and 1904. The old woman in the left center of the sheet, crouching with her arms folded, suggests the many versions of similar figures in Picasso's work of 1902 and 1903. The curious head at the lower left, as well as the egg-like form to the right of the feet of the standing woman in the center are reminiscent of details in a 1902 drawing in which similar forms appear.[2] For these reasons, it can be supposed that the sketch was probably made in Barcelona in 1902 or 1903.

A relationship among several of the more boldly drawn figures can be discerned, suggesting a *flamenco tablao*,[3] with singers, a dancer, and spectators. Two seated singers are at the right; one of them, whose song is indicated by lines emitting from his mouth, faces the dancing man at the left. Two smaller figures, one wearing a cap and smoking a cigarette and the other at his feet, are spectators of the dance. Picasso completes the circle with a profile of an older man at the upper left, and the head of a young woman at the upper center, who is in the company of an old *celestina*, a Spanish procuress.

Although the sketch has distinctly separate along with related figures, some more defined by ink and wash than others, there are unifying elements, particularly the various signatures of Picasso over the entire sheet. Furthermore, Picasso completes the lower right and the right margins with the faint tracing of female nudes. This bordering, exemplified especially by the reclining nude in the lower margin, is a compositional technique that returns frequently in the late graphic work of the artist, such as *Suite 347* of 1968.

1 Junyer-Vidal is discussed further under no. 33 in this catalogue.
2 Z.XXI.37.
3 A *flamenco tablao* is a stage performance with Andalusian music and dancing.

Private collection

Ca. 1902–03; signed twelve times: *Picasso* (ten times), *Yo Picasso* (one time), *Yo el Rey* (one time). Ink, wash, and pencil on paper; 28.0 x 38.1 cm.

Provenance: acquired in Paris in 1927.

33 *Sebastià Junyer-Vidal and Woman in a Café*
Portrait du peintre Sebastià Junyer-Vidal

In this beautifully composed painting of 1903, Picasso depicts his great friend, the painter Sebastià Junyer-Vidal, seated in a café with an unidentified woman. The artificial lighting of the room casts a hue suggesting the "green hour" of café life, the hour of the absinthe drinkers.

Both figures are directly facing the viewer, with Junyer-Vidal in the central position. The woman's facial features are boldly simplified, accentuating her large eyes and the deep shadows that sculpt the area of her neck and chest. The bluish skin tones of both figures contrast with the pink of Junyer-Vidal's lips and the orange-red flower in the woman's hair. A round table "floats" in front of the couple, and the thinly painted glass pitcher and drinking glass allow the oval contour of the tabletop to be seen as an unbroken curve, echoing the shape of Junyer-Vidal's head. At the lower right, the outline of Junyer-Vidal's hand directs the viewer's eye to Picasso's dedication to his friend Sebastian Juñer, using the Spanish spelling of the Catalan's name.

Sebastià and his brother Carles, a writer and critic, were frequent visitors to Els Quatre Gats after the turn of the century. The two brothers had inherited from their uncle a yarn and stocking shop in Barcelona, where Picasso spent long hours in conversation and making drawings on large sheets of paper from the store.[1] Between the years 1901, when their close friendship began, and 1904, Picasso portrayed Junyer-Vidal in at least twenty different drawings and paintings. Sebastià and Picasso made two trips together to Paris during the Quatre Gats years, the first in 1901 and again in 1904. During the first trip Picasso drew his delightful parody of Manet's *Olympia*, depicting Junyer-Vidal and himself in the presence of a negroid "Olympia."[2] Their second trip is documented by Picasso's *Aleluyas* (Museo Picasso, Barcelona), a charming pictorial narrative of the journey, one scene of which depicts Junyer-Vidal receiving a sack of money from the art dealer Durand-Ruel in Paris. Junyer-Vidal had earlier gained some public recognition in Barcelona for his talents as a painter. In October 1902 his first exhibition at the Sala Parés, in which he showed canvases representing the Majorcan countryside, was enthusiastically praised in *Catalunya Artística*,[3] and he had a second exhibition at the gallery in January 1904. After the Quatre Gats group dispersed, Junyer-Vidal devoted his energies to his art collection, which was housed in his museum-residence at Vallcarca, not far from Rusiñol's Cau Ferrat in Sitges.

Picasso's 1903 *Sebastià Junyer-Vidal and Woman in a Café*, the date of

Los Angeles County Museum of Art, Bequest of David E. Bright (M.67.25.18)

1903; inscribed, signed, and dated lower right: *A Sebastian Juñer, Picasso, Junio 1903*.
Oil on canvas; 126.4 x 94.0 cm.

Provenance: Sebastià Junyer-Vidal, Barcelona; Carlos and Xavier Junyer, Perpignan; Frank Gabriel Dereppe, Lugano; David E. Bright, Los Angeles.

Bibliography: Z.I.174; Daix IX.21; Cirici, *Picasso avant Picasso*, ill. opp. 80; Palau Fabre, *Picasso en Cataluña*, 110, ill. 97; Palau Fabre, *Picasso i els seus amics catalans*, 136; Lecaldano, Paolo, *The Complete Paintings of Picasso*, London, 1971, 93, ill. 72.

Exhibitions: Galerie Georges Petit, Paris, 1932, *Picasso*, no. 16; Museum of Modern Art, New York, 1957, *Picasso, 75th Anniversary Exhibition*, no. 18; Philadelphia Museum of Art, 1958, *Picasso*, no. 11; University of California at Los Angeles, 1961, *"Bonne Fête" Monsieur Picasso*, no. 4; Grand Palais, Paris, 1966, *Hommage à Pablo Picasso*, no. 17; Los Angeles County Museum of Art, 1967, *David E. Bright Collection*, 25; University Art Museum, University of California, Berkeley, 1970–71, *Excellence: Art from the University Community*, no. 537; Los Angeles County Museum of Art, 1975, *A Decade of Collecting 1965–1975*, 206–7, no. 100.

1 Palau Fabre, *Picasso i els seus amics catalans*, 129.
2 Daix IV.7.
3 F. Giraldós, "Artistas joves de Catalunya," *Catalunya Artística* (Oct. 1902), 477.

which coincides with Junyer-Vidal's growing fame, is an updated version of the earlier "Olympia" depiction of Sebastià, with Junyer-Vidal now in a café in the company of a Spanish prostitute. Although there are stylistic simplifications in the overall compositional structure of the painting and in the two figures, Junyer-Vidal's portrait is quite faithful to life. A photograph of the painter published in the October 1902 issue of *Catalunya Artística*, when Junyer-Vidal had the first exhibition of his paintings, shows the remarkable accuracy of Picasso's portrayal of his friend.

34 *Family at Supper*
Evocation of Horta de Ebro

Fond memories of several months spent in an Aragonese village, Horta de Ebro, in 1898, suggested a number of drawings on the general theme of Spanish life and customs that Picasso developed in Barcelona in 1903.[1] This watercolor depicts a family at mealtime in a simple country interior. The man at the left, seen from behind, is dressed in the style of a peasant, a *campesino* (note his cummerbund and vest), and grasps a *porrón*, the Spanish wine flask, in the center of the composition. The standing woman at the right, with her head covered in a traditional manner, places a bowl on the table in front of the seated child, who is also seen from the back. There is a suggestion of silent and familiar ritual in this subtly rendered drawing, conveyed by Picasso's simplification of forms and gestures in the carefully constructed interior scene. The drawing reflects the artist's interest at the time in patterns of human life, and the family in particular.

1 See Daix IX.13–16, IX.18–21.

Albright-Knox Art Gallery, Buffalo, Room of Contemporary Art Fund (RCA41:3)

1903; signed lower right: *Picasso*. Watercolor and ink on paper; 31.7 x 43.2 cm.

Provenance: Gertrude Stein, Paris; Galerie Kate Perls, Paris; Peter Watson, London; French Art Galleries, New York.

Bibliography: Z.VI.563; Daix IX.13; *Magazine of Art*, vol. 34, no. 7, 1941, 384; *Catalogue of Contemporary Painting and Sculpture*, Albright Art Gallery, Buffalo Fine Arts Academy, 1949, 94–95; Cirici, *Picasso avant Picasso*, ill. 143 (as *Le Repas des laboureurs*); Kay, Helen, *Picasso's World of Children*, New York, 1965, 52; Palau Fabre, *Picasso en Cataluña*, ill. 94; Burns, Edward, ed., *Gertrude Stein on Picasso*, New York, 1970, 12; Lecaldano, Paolo, *The Complete Paintings of Picasso*, London, 1971, 93, ill. 81 (as *Family at Table*); DeNitto, Dennis, *Media for Our Time*, New York, 1971, 368; Newman, Barbara M. and Newman, Philip R., *Development through Life*, Homewood, Ill., 1975, 299.

Exhibitions: Yale University Art Gallery, New Haven, 1951, *Pictures for a Picture of Gertrude Stein*, no. 26; Milwaukee Art Institute, 1957, no. 82.

Pablo Picasso

35 Sign for Els Quatre Gats

This metal sign, attributed to Picasso, once hung above the main entrance to Els Quatre Gats on Calle Montesión. The design cleverly suggests the name of "The Four Cats" by the differentiation in color, for the two arched cats are painted black on one side and gray on the other. The late owner of the sign, Manuel Rocamora, suggested that its designer was the young Picasso.[1] If this is the case, the mobile would have to date after the artist began to participate regularly in café activities in late 1898.

1 Interview with Rocamora, 26 January 1968, Barcelona.

Fundación Manuel Rocamora, Barcelona

1898–99.
Painted metal (two parts); 35 x 34 cm.

Ramón Pichot Gironés
1870–1925

After studying at La Llotja, Pichot spent much of his time assisting Rusiñol with various *modernista* activities in Sitges during the 1890s. Three works by Pichot were included in the first Quatre Gats exhibition in 1897, and a one-man show was held at the café in 1899. After the turn of the century, Pichot lived primarily in Paris and exhibited frequently in Barcelona, Madrid, and the French salons. His friendship with Picasso continued through their Parisian years until Pichot's death in the French capital in 1925.

36 Illustration for *Fulls de la vida* by Santiago Rusiñol

Rusiñol's literary work, *Fulls de la vida*, was published in 1898, with illustrations by Pichot. A collection of reminiscences from the "pages of life," it reveals its symbolist inspiration in the highly evocative language and imagery that Rusiñol employs. The present drawing, with its fantastic, intertwined beasts and humans, relates specifically to the chapter "Els amics del sostre." The passage that inspired Pichot describes the creatures that inhabit the ceiling, actually the imagination of Rusiñol, who lies ill in bed below:

> I began to become engulfed in those islands [on the ceiling]; I explored the terrain and soon figures began to emerge, entire figures, veiled women, knights in capes, armed warriors, sirens (of the rain), fantastic fish and dragons with wings, and apocalyptic monsters. . . .[1]

When Rusiñol recovers from the hallucinatory moments of his illness, the ceiling is freshly painted and returns once more to a simple, blank surface of his room, like a new canvas awaiting the artist's hand.

Pichot's own symbolism derives from the tradition of artists such as Odilon Redon, for whom the illustrations themselves could convey moods similar to the passages that they accompanied. The qualities of darkness and glowing light of the drawings for *Fulls de la vida*, in addition to the specific figurative imagery, thus contribute to their evocative power.

1 Rusiñol, *Obres completes*, 138.

Cau Ferrat, Sitges

1898.
Drawing for publication, conté crayon on paper; 27 x 29.6 cm.

Bibliography: Jordà, Josep Maria, *La Publicidad* (Nov. 1898); Cirici, *El arte modernista catalán*, 375.

37 *Boulevard at Sunset*
Boulevard de Paris al atardecer

Pichot's choice of late evening light contributes to the evocative mood of this composition; lights on the boulevard flicker and a gas lamp glows at the right, while at the back the last glimmer of daylight takes on a serpentine shape. The open foreground accentuates the wide boulevard, and the figures seem to be placed randomly against this space. *Boulevard at Sunset* was probably painted in Paris, where Pichot moved in about 1900. Prior to this date, most of the oils referred to in catalogues and in reviews of his exhibitions deal with the subject of the Spanish landscape and the Mediterranean seaside.

Cau Ferrat, Sitges

Ca. 1900; signed: *R. Pichot*; verso: painting of woman seen in profile. Oil on canvas; 68 x 55 cm.

Bibliography: Sitges, *Catálogo de pintura y dibujo del "Cau Ferrat,"* 29.

Santiago Rusiñol Prats
1861–1931

Santiago Rusiñol, one of the founders of Els Quatre Gats, was a productive and gregarious individual whose interests ranged from painting to writing, collecting, and traveling. Rusiñol was from a wealthy Catalan family and had first studied painting with Tomás Moragas in Barcelona. Later he attended classes at the Académie Gervex in Paris, where Gervex, Humbert, Carrière, and Puvis de Chavannes were "correctors." Rusiñol's activities as a collector, particularly of medieval ironwork, led to the founding of a small museum, the Cau Ferrat, in 1885 in Barcelona, and to the *modernista* gathering place of the same name inaugurated in Sitges in 1894. Rusiñol divided his time between Paris, Barcelona, and Sitges from 1889 to the late 1890s. In France he acted as a correspondent for *La Vanguardia*, and he also frequently exhibited paintings there and in Spain. Certainly the impact of the *modernista* movement on painting, and to some extent on Catalan literature, can be traced to Rusiñol's varied activities during this period. After the turn of the century, he directed his energies to writing and painting, particularly to the subject of Spanish gardens.

38 *Portrait of Miguel Utrillo*

Rusiñol's *Portrait of Miguel Utrillo* was painted in Paris in 1890 and shows the artist, puppeteer, and aspiring critic at the entrance to the garden of the Moulin de la Galette. Beyond the gates are the familiar lanterns of the garden, and to the right in the foreground are plants and a large bust, which decorate an interior courtyard. This canvas is the second of two full-length portraits Rusiñol painted of Utrillo at the Moulin de la Galette, and contrasts with the gray, bare setting of the other.[1]

In several respects, Rusiñol's 1891 portrait typifies the artist's attitude towards naturalism, which Barcelona critics saw as one of his major contributions to the *nova escola* of Catalan painting. The naturalistic approach signified that all elements of a given composition were given equal attention, be they figures or landscape surroundings, and an attempt was made to capture the effects of light and atmosphere. Here the viewer's eye is indeed led to all areas of the composition, both to the figure, whose pose suggests contemporary photographic portraiture, and to the surroundings. Color and a loosened brush stroke animate the overall surface, most vividly in the area of the plant stand to the right. Atmospheric qualities of the background are suggested by a greenish tonality, not unlike the subdued, misty background of Casas's *Portrait of Erik Satie* [8] of the following year. Although this idea of painterly naturalism was already well established in France, its interpretation by Rusiñol and Casas was important to the development of *modernismo* as a Catalan style in the 1890s.

1 Rusiñol's other *Portrait of Miguel Utrillo* (Museo de Arte Moderno, Barcelona) was exhibited in both the Champ de Mars salon (illustrated in the catalogue as no. 791) and the Salon Meissonier in Paris in 1890.

Museo de Arte Moderno, Barcelona

1890; signed lower right: *S. Rusiñol*. Oil on canvas; 193 x 129 cm.

Provenance: heirs of Miguel Utrillo; acquired in 1945.

Bibliography: Cirici, *El arte modernista catalán*, 337; Rusiñol, *Obres completes*, pl. 12; Rusiñol, Maria, *Santiago Rusiñol vist per la seva filla*, pl. 4; Jardí, *Història de Els 4 Gats*, 27; Cervera, *Modernismo*, ill. 53.

S. Rusiñol

39 *Paris Studio*
Taller de Paris

Paris Studio is actually a double portrait of Suzanne Valadon and Miguel Utrillo seen in a closed room. Utrillo, dressed in a gray suit and light-colored hat, reclines upon the bed along the back wall. In the foreground at the left, Valadon, wearing a dark street dress and a lavender flowered hat, is holding a white object (perhaps a letter that she is reading). Rusiñol's figures do not communicate, yet they fill the space of the darkened interior. The mood of this scene is suggestive of quiet intimacy, enhanced by the choice of subdued colors and the closed structure of the composition. In this way, *Paris Studio* relates to an "intimist" trend in the early 1890s discernible in the work of painters such as the Nabi Vuillard and Casas (see, for example, the latter's *Anxiety* [9]).

Utrillo and Valadon had first met in 1883 at Le Chat Noir on the occasion of a two-hour lecture and demonstration given by Utrillo concerning the Ball del Ciri ("candle dance"), a dance performed in the church by outgoing church wardens.[1] Impressed by the energetic Catalan, Valadon made his acquaintance and the two artists were seen in each other's company regularly that year, until Utrillo left in the fall for travels that took him to Bulgaria, Germany, and Belgium. When Valadon gave birth to her son Maurice on 26 December 1883, friends assumed Utrillo to be the father. It was not, however, until 1891 (the date of Rusiñol's painting) that Utrillo signed an official act of recognition that the child was his own.[2]

1 Storm, *The Valadon Drama*, 62.

2 Valadon insisted throughout her life that she was uncertain as to the paternity of the child. Nevertheless, upon seeing a photograph of Miguel at the time of his death in 1934, she admitted in an interview with Berthe Weil that he was, indeed, the father of Maurice (Storm, *The Valadon Drama*, 99). For a further discussion supporting the position that Miguel Utrillo was Maurice's natural father, see Banlin-Lacroix, "Miguel Utrillo i Morlius: critique d'art," 35–42.

Collection of Manuel Garí de Arana, Barcelona

1891; signed lower right: *S. Rusiñol.* Oil on canvas; 39 x 62 cm.

Provenance: Establecimientos Maragall, S.A.

Bibliography: McCully, "Els Quatre Gats," 1975, 39, 244–45, ill. 6.

Exhibition: Sala Parés, Barcelona, 1971–72, *La época del Sr. Parés*, no. 2.

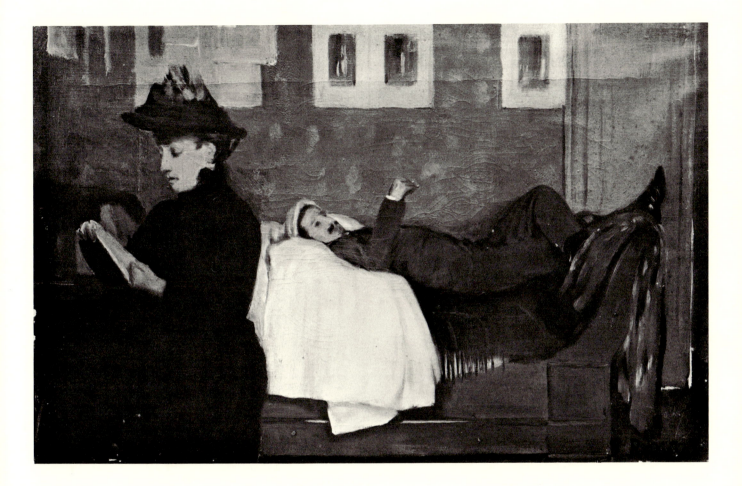

40 *Outskirts of Paris*
Arrabal de Paris

This is the second of two compositions by Rusiñol for which the painters Suzanne Valadon and Miguel Utrillo served as models, the other being the interior, *Paris Studio* [39]. Here the couple is seen on a hillside; Valadon is seated just to the left of the center and Utrillo, wearing a uniform borrowed from their mutual friend Erik Satie, is lying on his stomach to her right. Rusiñol allows the foreground to occupy almost two-thirds of the canvas, emphasizing the sense of a steep incline upon which the two figures are situated. Behind them are a few scattered structures and the familiar windmills of Montmartre.

Museo de Arte Moderno, Barcelona

1891; signed lower right: *S. Rusiñol.*
Oil on canvas; 48.5 x 72 cm.

Provenance: Martin Estany; acquired in 1936.

Bibliography: Ráfols, *Modernismo y modernistas*, ill. 18 (as *Utrillo y Suzanne Valadon en Montmartre*); Rusiñol, *Obres completes*, pl. 14; Castillo, Alberto, "Crónica de Barcelona," *Goya*, no. 93 (Nov.–Dec. 1969), 180; McCully, "Els Quatre Gats," 1975, 38–39, ill. 5.

Exhibitions: Sala Parés, Barcelona, 1891, no. 40 (as *En campaña, Utrillo & Valadon*); Sala Parés, Barcelona, 1969, *Exposición Homenaje a Santiago Rusiñol*, no. 4; Museo de Arte Moderno, Barcelona, 1974, *El impresionismo en España*, no. 64.

Santiago Rusiñol

4I *Interior of a Café*

In 1892, when he exhibited *Interior of a Café* at the Champ de Mars, Santiago Rusiñol was no longer a stranger to the Parisian art world. He had become familiar with the bohemian life of Montmartre and had overcome the initially dizzying diversity of the French capital. Moreover, by 1892 official recognition had been achieved, for in that year he joined his compatriot Ramón Casas as an *associé* of the Société Nationale des Beaux-Arts.

Interior of a Café was one of six works exhibited by Rusiñol at the Salon that year. It was purchased less than a week after the opening of the exhibition by A. Harrison for John G. Johnson of Philadelphia. The work, number 899 in the exhibition catalogue, was there entitled *Un Aquarium*, possibly referring to the name of the café depicted.[1] Its present title derives from the one under which it was exhibited at the Union League in Philadelphia a year later.

In his illustrated *Salon de 1892*, Hustin describes the work in his short comment on Rusiñol:

> Mr. Rusiñol,—qui est d'origine espagnole,—a mis lui aussi beaucoup d'esprit à nous conter comment, dans certains cabarets borgnes, des femmes interlopes attendent le client, dans une salle dont le demijour favorise leur petit commerce.[2]

Hustin's remarks about obscure bars and clandestine women awaiting their clientele in the half-light suggest that, for the late-nineteenth-century Parisian, *Interior of a Café* was noteworthy for its social content. Yet, as with many of Rusiñol's works, the painting's essence is the expression of a mood—in this case, that of the seated woman to the left. As in Rusiñol's *Bohemian* (1891, Maragall Collection, Barcelona), the room in which she sits echoes her silent, lethargic melancholy.[3] In the earlier work, Rusiñol accomplished this through the harmonious amplification of the figure's mood by the environment. In *Interior of a Café*, her mood pervades the foreground and is reinforced by the contrast of the latter with the brighter and livelier background.

This more complex pictorial structure results in the introduction of an unusually large number of actors for a painting by Rusiñol. However, only the seated woman possesses any psychological vitality, and meaningful interaction between individuals is carefully avoided. (*Pentimenti* in the area of the seated male in the back room betray Rusiñol's efforts to isolate him

John G. Johnson Collection, Philadelphia

1892; signed lower right: *S. Rusiñol*. Oil on canvas; 100.3 x 81.92 cm.

Provenance: acquired from the Champ de Mars Salon, 1892.

Bibliography: Hustin, A., *Salon de 1892*, Paris, 1892, 86; *Catalogue of a Collection of Paintings Belonging to John G. Johnson*, Philadelphia, 1892; Valentiner, Willem R., *Catalogue of a Collection of Paintings and Some Art Objects*, vol. 3, Philadelphia, 1914, no. 1078; *Catalogue of John G. Johnson Collection*, Philadelphia Museum of Art, 1941, 66.

Exhibitions: Salon de Champ de Mars, Paris, 1892, no. 899 (as *Un Aquarium*); Union League, Philadelphia, 1893, no. 100 (as *Interior of Drinking Café*).

---

1 In the receipt given to Harrison, the painting is identified by number and called *L'Aquarium*, which makes this possibility even more likely.

2 A. Hustin, *Salon de 1892: Société des artistes français et Société Nationale des Beaux-Arts*, 86.

3 Rusiñol, *Obres completes*, pl. 11.

S. Rusiñol

from the man moving across the doorway.) The bold cropping of figures, the recession through successive spaces, and the subject matter of *Interior of a Café* all recall late-nineteenth-century Parisian art, specifically that of Degas (*Cotton Market, New Orleans*, 1873, Musée des Beaux-Arts, Pau; and *Absinthe*, 1876, Louvre, Paris). Yet it is precisely when we compare the painting with a work such as *Absinthe* that we note Rusiñol's unique adaptation of Parisian artistic innovations. With the aid of absinthe, Degas's woman sinks within herself and sits oblivious to the activity within the café. Her pathetic melancholy derives from her utter isolation from her environment. On the other hand, the potency of the woman's melancholy in Rusiñol's painting derives from the reflection of her mood by the environment. Contrast is employed to intensify the atmosphere, but the unity of the figure and its setting, that quality of *poésie* lauded by Rusiñol's Barcelona critics, remains the fundamental characteristic of the work.   R.M.

42   *The Morphine Addict*
La morfina

Rusiñol worked on *The Morphine Addict* in Paris in 1894, a year of varied stylistic experimentation for the artist.[1] However, when the painting was exhibited in October of that year in Barcelona, the bold, tightly structured interior surprised critics, who expected the ashen palette of the Parisian settings of Rusiñol's earlier work. Although the subject contrasts with the quiet, enigmatic interiors of the early 1890s, such as *Paris Studio* [39], its inspiration can also be traced to artistic sources outside of Spain.

The painting shows an addict lying in bed, clutching at the bedclothes over her, as she waits for the dose of morphine to transport her to a dream world and dull her sensations. Illness and the world of drugs were current themes in late-nineteenth-century "symbolist" and "decadent" literature, drama, and painting.[2] Rusiñol's interest was in part personal, for he took morphine during those years to treat a chronic illness. However, his debt to European symbolism became more evident, particularly in his literary production, at approximately the time he painted *The Morphine Addict*. His inaugural speech at the opening of the Cau Ferrat in 1894, for example, was overladen with symbolist imagery and suggestion.[3] It is important to

Cau Ferrat, Sitges

1894; signed lower right: *S. Rusiñol*. Oil on canvas; 87.3 x 115 cm.

Bibliography: *La Renaixensa* (18 Oct. 1894); *La Publicidad* (19 Oct. 1894); *Diario de Barcelona* (25 Oct. 1894); "Exposició Santiago Rusiñol," *La Veu de Catalunya* (18 Oct. 1894), 493–94; Tobar, Alfonso, "Santiago Rusiñol," *Gil Blas*, 1894, see Archivo Rusiñol, vol. 3, 14; *Pèl & Ploma* (Sept. 1901), 100; Sitges, *Catálogo de pintura y dibujo del "Cau Ferrat,"* 38; Sitges, *Guía sumaria del Cau Ferrat*, 82; Cirici, *El arte modernista catalán*, 82; Blunt and Pool, *Picasso*, ill. 44; Maragall, *Història de la Sala Parés*, ill. 43; McCully, "Els Quatre Gats," 1975, 99–100, ill. 12; Cervera, *Modernismo*, ill. 168.

Exhibitions: Sala Parés, Barcelona, 1894; Sala Parés, Barcelona, 1969, *Exposición Homenaje Santiago Rusiñol*, no. 16.

1 It was also in 1894 that Rusiñol painted the first two decorative allegories, *La pintura* and *La poesia*, for the Cau Ferrat. Inspired by Puvis de Chavannes, fifteenth-century Italian painting, and to some extent art-nouveau decoration, they were a definite departure from the "realism" of Rusiñol's early work.

2 Blunt and Pool have related *The Morphine Addict* to the decadent theme of the artist Edvard Munch's *The Morning After* of 1894 (National Gallery, Oslo); they also mention the drug imagery in Rusiñol's writing, including *El pati blau* and "La casa del silenci" (see *Picasso*, ills. 44–45).

3 *Festa Modernista del Cau Ferrat, Certamen Literari, Tercer any, celebrat a Sitges el 4 de novembre de 1894*, Barcelona, 1894.

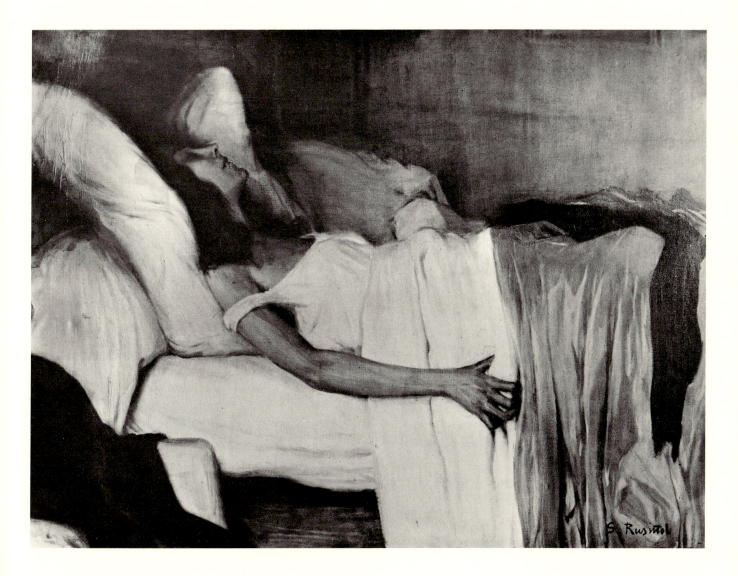

note that the importation of symbolist themes by artists such as Rusiñol had an impact on the Catalan art movement in general, and accounts for the "decadence" ascribed to *modernista* writers and artists beginning in the mid-1890s.

A comparison of *The Morphine Addict* with *The Medal* (fig. 20), a canvas by Rusiñol of approximately the same date and size, shows the contrasting moods created by the artist, using the same model and interior. In *The Medal*, the woman is sitting up in bed and examining a gleaming gold medal. The contemplative mood of the scene, closer to *Paris Studio* [39], is achieved by her posture and by a general softening of the interior coloration. In *The Morphine Addict*, the gripping, dramatic quality is due both to the woman's position and to the bold simplification of forms and the contrast of stark bright areas with saturated darks.

20 Santiago Rusiñol. *The Medal* (*La medalla*), oil on canvas, 1894. Cau Ferrat, Sitges

43 Poster: *L'alegria que passa*

Rusiñol's poster advertised his one-act play, *L'alegria que passa*, with music by Enric Morera, which was presented at Adrià Gual's Teatre Intim in Barcelona in 1898. The play was well received and was produced again in Barcelona in 1901 in three versions: in the original Catalan at the Teatre Tivoli, in Italian at the Teatre Novetats, and in Castilian at the Eldorado. The work was also translated into French. Moreover, the first issue of *Pèl & Ploma* (3 June 1899) was dedicated to the play and included drawings by Rusiñol and Casas of the various types portrayed.

The theme of *L'alegria que passa* is suggested in the poster. The clown, a member of a troupe of traveling entertainers, symbolizes personal freedom. He walks on the open road among scattered leaves (likened to bohemian songs in the play), ahead of the wagon that carries the other performers. Their transient life contrasts with the social confinement of the small towns where they perform. The *saltimbanques* try to bring a little gladness into the boring lives of their audiences; yet their own existence is a lonely one, for they must keep traveling and leave these moments of happiness behind.

The life of the wandering performer, which Rusiñol greatly popularized in *L'alegria que passa*, complemented a general interest among *modernista* writers and artists in marginal groups, such as Nonell's cretins or Canals's gypsies. The itinerant entertainer was adopted as a subject by several of the Quatre Gats group, notably Opisso and Picasso. In fact, the spirit of Rusiñol's play can be linked to Picasso's studies of *saltimbanques* of 1904–05.

Museo de Arte Escénico, Barcelona

1898; signed in stone lower left: *S. Rusiñol*; printer's notation: *Tirat a Can Utrillo & Rialp Passeig de Gracia 174 Barna.*
Lithograph; 85.5 x 55 cm.

Bibliography: Deschamps, "L'Affiche espagnole," 240, ill. 10; *La Vanguardia* (15 July 1899); Santos Torroella, *El cartel*, 31; Ráfols, "Los carteles '1900,'" 35–36; Montsalvatge, Xavier, "La música y los músicos del modernismo en la Barcelona de traspaso de siglo," *Destino* (25 Oct. 1969), 55.

Exhibition: Casón del Buen Retiro, Madrid, 1969, *El modernismo en España*, no. v-18.

Joaquim Sunyer Miró
1875–1958

Sunyer was born in Sitges and in 1889 moved with his family to Barcelona, where he was enrolled in art classes at La Llotja. His companions in the early 1890s included the artists Nonell and Mir, among others. In 1894 Sunyer moved to Paris, where he lived for many years. At the Bateau Lavoir his residence coincided with that of Picasso, who moved there in 1904. Although Sunyer was absent from the majority of Quatre Gats activities in Barcelona, his friendship with members of the group was an important link for Catalan artists with Parisian art circles.

44 Illustrations for *Les Soliloques du pauvre* by Jehan Rictus

The lithographs accompany Jehan Rictus's collection of poems *Les Soliloques du pauvre*, which describe the thoughts and tribulations of a Parisian tramp. Eight of the poems are illustrated: "L'Hiver," "Impressions de Promenade," "Songe-Mensonge," "Le Revenant," "Les Soliloques du Chanteur Ambulant," "Epilogue," "Farandole des Pauv's Tits Fans-Fans," and "Le Printemps."

The protagonist in all the illustrations is the *pauvre*, the "poor man," clad in a shabby frock coat and top hat. This is possibly a rendering of the author himself, who had lived in Paris as a tramp for a while, before he became famous in 1896 by reciting his poems first at the Café des Quat-z-Arts and subsequently at Rodolphe Salis's Le Chat Noir.

Themes from the life of the poor and the disinherited, the cast-outs of industrialized society and of the big cities, had been popular in most countries both in literature and in painting since the middle of the nineteenth century. Novels and poems made fashionable a new type of hero, the city tramp, a wretched counterpart to Baudelaire's *flâneur* and brother to similar characters by Gorki and Pio Baroja.

Sunyer's interest in such themes must have been stimulated by the Parisian milieu in which he lived and more particularly by the art of the Swiss graphic artist Théophile-Alexandre Steinlen (1859–1923), then at the height of his career. Steinlen, a confirmed socialist, regularly contributed illustrations inspired from Parisian street life to leftist newspapers. He had also illustrated Salis's review *Le Chat Noir*, Aristide Bruant's collection of songs *Dans la rue* (1889), and Rictus's *Soliloques*. In fact, Sunyer's illustrations for this book are related both in inspiration and style to those of Steinlen, which closely preceded them. N.M.A.

Private collection

1897.
Illustrated book in 8°; 22 x 17 cm. Contains eight color lithographs, with a portrait of the author on the cover by Sunyer and a second portrait of the author on the frontispiece by T. A. Steinlen, signed and dated December 1895. Two hundred copies of this book were printed on China paper and published at Pierre Dufand's, 25, galerie Vivienne, Paris, 1897. This is copy no. 24.

Provenance: Lecomte, Paris, 1972.

Bibliography: de Crauzat, E., *L'Oeuvre gravé et lithographié de Steinlen*, Paris, 1913, 159, no. 595 (the book is catalogued without reference to Sunyer); *Exposición Joaquim Sunyer*, Barcelona, 1959, 9.

Joaquim Sunyer

45 Woman at Her Toilet
La Toilette

Formerly attributed to Picasso, this pastel by Joaquim Sunyer shows a special interest on the part of the Spaniards in Paris for late-nineteenth-century French subjects and the medium of pastel, made popular by Degas and other artists. Sunyer's nude is depicted bathing in the privacy of her room. The figure is seen in profile, parallel to the picture plane, and contrasts with the generally flattened space behind her. Warm pastel colors, particularly in the vase and painting on the wall, are used to surround the figure and accentuate the softened contours of her body. A shadow beneath her and next to the white water-pitcher stabilizes her position two-dimensionally in the composition. Picasso's interest in the subject, also inspired by French sources and perhaps even by Sunyer, generally dates from his second visit to Paris in 1901 and can be seen in works such as *The Blue Room* (Phillips Collection, Washington, D.C.).

Sunyer himself is responsible for the previously mistaken attribution of this work, for in the presence of Jaime Sabartés, Sunyer painted over his own signature and replaced it below with the name Picasso.[1] This must have been done some time after 1930, for it was photographed as a Sunyer pastel by the art photographer Serra that year, when the work was in the Benet Collection in Barcelona.

1 I am indebted for this information to Mr. Juan Ainaud Lasarte, Director, Museos de Arte de Barcelona, who learned of the incident from Jaime Sabartés.

John A. and Audrey Jones Beck Collection, Houston

Ca. 1900; signed middle left: *Picasso*; originally signed upper middle left: *Sunyer*; verso: drawing of head of a woman.
Pastel, pencil, and wash on cardboard; 26.7 x 27.9 cm.

Provenance: Benet Collection, Barcelona (as Sunyer); Mr. and Mrs. Herbert L. Matthews, New York, 1964 (as Picasso); Sotheby and Co., London, 1964 (as Picasso).

Bibliography (as Picasso): Z.VI.397; Daix IV.17; Houston, *The Collection of John A. and Audrey Jones Beck, Impressionist and Post-Impressionist Paintings*, 1974, 72.

Exhibition: Museum of Fine Arts, Houston, 1973, *Pablo Picasso, 1881–1973: A Memorial Exhibition*, no. 1 (as Picasso).

46 *Sentimental Promenade*
Promenade sentimentale

Almost two-thirds of *Sentimental Promenade* is a mass of reddish-brown foliage; highlights fall on the faces of the figures, whose placement in the foreground and in the distance creates a sense of spatial vastness appropriate to the large park. This etching probably belongs to the same series as *Conversation in the Park* [47].   D.H.

Private collection

1900; signed lower right: *Sunyer*.
Etching with aquatint; 32 x 21 cm.

Provenance: Lecomte, Paris, 1972.

11/25   Sunyer.

Joaquim Sunyer

47 *Conversation in the Park*
Conversation au grand public

Sunyer's etching represents people in a public garden. Prominence is given to the group in the foreground, seated in a circle, their heads brought together as if engaged in animated conversation. A few more groups are set in the right and left background, balancing the central element; there is a group of seated women on the right, and on the left, a pair of lovers and a strolling couple.

The scene takes place in a Paris park, perhaps the Tuileries or the Luxembourg, which were favored leisure haunts of the Parisians of the time. In theme it carries on the impressionist tradition and that of paintings of "modern life," such as Manet's well-known *Concert in the Tuileries Garden* (1862, National Gallery, London).

During his long stay in Paris, Sunyer was closely associated with the post-impressionist artistic climate. Indeed, the character of intimacy that emanates from this scene, as well as certain stylistic features, can be traced to the influence of Bonnard and Vuillard. Moreover, the stylization of the forms and a certain decorative, almost caricatural treatment of the contours indicate familiarity with the art of Toulouse-Lautrec and Forain.

The etching is dedicated to the artist's friend Eugène Delâtre, the engraver who became popular in the 1890s for his color prints of lively Parisian outdoor life and picturesque views of Montmartre.   N.M.A.

Private collection

1900; inscribed and signed lower right: *A mon bon ami Delâtre, Sunyer.* Etching with aquatint, proof of first state, before block at lower right; 18.5 x 21.5 cm.

Provenance: Lecomte, Paris, 1972.

Miguel Utrillo Morlius
1862–1934

Prior to his role in the founding of Els Quatre Gats, Miguel Utrillo first began a career in engineering in Barcelona and in science writing on the staff of *Revista internacional de ciencia* (1879–80). In 1880 Utrillo moved to Paris, where he was admitted to the Institut National Agronomique. However, his real interests lay in the cabaret life of Montmartre and he was soon included in the circle of Le Chat Noir. At Salis's famed establishment, Utrillo learned the art of shadow puppet theater and there met the French model and painter Suzanne Valadon in 1883. Her son Maurice, who was born in December of that year, later took Utrillo's name when Miguel signed an official act of paternal recognition in 1891. After travels in Bulgaria, Germany, and Belgium, Utrillo spent two years in Barcelona before returning to Paris in 1889. From 1889 to 1893 Utrillo worked as a correspondent for the Barcelona daily *La Vanguardia*, using both the pseudonym Lile and his own name. Among his Catalan friends he was called Sr. Domingo; later in the 1890s he also used the pseudonyms A. L. de Baran, P. de X., and Pinzell. For a period in 1891 Utrillo ran his own shadow puppet theater in the Auberge du Clou on Avenue Trudaine in Paris, where the musician was Erik Satie. In 1893 Utrillo went to Chicago, where he worked in a Parisian shadow puppet theater and in the Fine Arts Section of the World's Columbian Exposition. After travel in the United States and Cuba and residence in New York, Utrillo returned to Barcelona in 1895. In the late 1890s he collaborated on activities at Rusiñol's Cau Ferrat in Sitges, and in Barcelona served as literary editor of *Pèl & Ploma* and later *Forma*. After the closing of Els Quatre Gats, Utrillo directed the construction of Mar-i-cel, Charles Deering's residence in Sitges. Utrillo's principal activities until his death in 1934 included collaboration on various journals as art critic and the direction of the construction of the Pueblo Español in Montjuich (1921–29).

48 *Parisian Fantasy*
Fantasia parisiense

Parisian Fantasy is one of only a few drawings by Utrillo that remain from the early 1890s. A combination of influences is at work in this rendering of a woman at an outdoor café on a hillside beneath a Montmartre windmill. In technique, it imitates the effects of printmaking. As if he were using his shadow puppets as models, Utrillo cut out and pinned some sections of the composition to the sheet of paper (pinholes are still visible in the area of the windmill). Then he spattered the sheet with ink, creating the effect of aquatint. This was done several times to produce the differing degrees of shading, contrasting with the white areas. Ink was used to emphasize the outline of the flat shapes. The silhouetted effect is reminiscent of Toulouse-Lautrec, as in the skirt fragment at the lower left, and of Ibels, particularly

Museo de Arte Moderno, Barcelona

Ca. 1890; inscribed and signed lower right: *A mon amich Casellas, Miguel Utrillo*; monogram combining the artist's initials *M* and *U* upper right. India ink on paper; 38.9 x 29.9 cm.

Provenance: Raimon Casellas.

Bibliography: *La Vanguardia* (1 Jan. 1897), 8.

Exhibition: Casón del Buen Retiro, Madrid, 1969, *El modernismo en España*, no. II-34.

À mon ami Casellas

Miguel Utrillo

in the figure above the skirt at the left. The sense of tipped-up space and the lantern with Utrillo's monogram in the upper right also reflect the Japanese influence on contemporary French poster and print design admired by Utrillo.

49 *Portrait of Suzanne Valadon*

This drawing was made during the period of reconciliation of the two artists Suzanne Valadon and Miguel Utrillo. The inscription, "In memory of the seven-year war," is a cryptic reference to the volatile years of their relationship between 1883, when Valadon's son was born, and 1891, when Utrillo recognized the child as his own.

Suzanne Valadon (ca. 1865–1938) had begun a career in the circus and then as an artist's model, and had worked for artists such as Puvis de Chavannes, Renoir, Toulouse-Lautrec, and Zandomeneghi. In the early 1890s, with an introduction from Toulouse-Lautrec, she met Degas who taught her printmaking and drawing. Valadon's personal contacts in Parisian art circles were important for Utrillo, who was becoming increasingly interested in writing art criticism. Valadon continued throughout her life to exhibit her paintings and drawings, often with her son Maurice Utrillo, and later with her husband André Utter.

Cau Ferrat, Sitges

1894; inscribed and dated lower right: *Record de la guerra dels set anys, Paris, 94*; monogram combining artist's initials *M* and *U* lower right. Conté crayon and sanguine on paper; 30.5 x 19.7 cm.

Bibliography: *Catálogo de pintura y dibujo del "Cau Ferrat,"* 46–47; Utrillo, "Las 'sombras chinescas' vistas por dentro" (28 April), 4.

Exhibition: Els Quatre Gats, Barcelona, 1897, *Breu relació dels dibuixos i estudis al oli fi que alguns pintors han exposat a la sala dels Quatre Gats,* no. 54.

Carlos Vázquez Ubeda
1869–1944

Carlos Vázquez, a painter from Ciudad Real, lived in Paris from 1889 to 1896 and studied with the painter Léon Bonnat. After moving to Barcelona in 1896, he worked as a painter and illustrator in the Catalan capital and exhibited at Els Quatre Gats in 1900. In addition, Vázquez's works were often featured at the Sala Parés and at official Spanish exhibitions.

50 *J. B. Parés*

This pastel drawing by the painter Carlos Vázquez served as the poster for the last exhibition of the year 1904 at the Sala Parés, organized by its founder Juan Bautista Parés. A woman and her young daughter are shown looking through what purports to be the display window of the Sala Parés on Petritxol, 3 y 5. However, Vázquez's source for the design is actually a Parisian storefront, which has been here adapted to fit the needs of the poster. A pastel by Vázquez, signed and dated 1904 in Paris (fig. 21), depicts the woman, accompanied by a tall man instead of the child, in the same attitude and looking at a very similar window display. A taller version of the clock has been moved farther to the right in the poster design, adding a vertical element lost by the removal of the male figure. In the poster Vázquez effectively touches the capes of the woman and the girl with white chalk (repeated on the flowers in the window), giving a lively quality to the overall design.

The art gallery Sala Parés was founded in 1877 and enlarged in a new building which opened in 1884 in its present location on Carrer Petritxol, near the Plaça del Pí in Barcelona's Barri Gótic. The gallery has served as an important force in the promotion of Catalan painting and sculpture.[1] In addition to shows of works by local artists, particularly Rusiñol, Casas, and their friend the sculptor Clarasó, during the 1890s, the gallery sponsored foreign poster exhibitions (1896, 1898) and other special events during the Quatre Gats years. Members of the café group were occasionally featured, notably Picasso, who exhibited a group of pastels there in 1901.

1 The earliest account of the Sala Parés is Enseñat's in *La Ilustración Catalana* in 1904. A record of the gallery's major contribution to the artistic history of the city up to the present day is Maragall's recent *Història de la Sala Parés*, 1975.

Establecimientos Maragall, S.A., Barcelona (28.095)

1904; signed and dated lower right: *Carlos Vázquez, 1904*. Pastel and charcoal on paper; 65 x 48 cm.

Bibliography: Maragall, *Història de la Sala Parés*, 98, ill. 84.

Exhibitions: Sala Parés, Barcelona, 1904; Sala Parés, Barcelona, 1950, *La época del Sr. Parés*; Casón del Buen Retiro, Madrid, 1969, *El modernismo en España*, no. V-21; Sala Parés, Barcelona, 1977.

21 Carlos Vázquez. Untitled pastel, Paris, 1904. Whereabouts unknown. Reproduced from *Album salon 1905: Revista Ibero-Americana de literatura y arte (1899–1907)*, 9

5I Sheet music with covers illustrated by Carles Maria Baró,
Lluis Bonnin, Adrià Gual, Joan Llimona, Jaume Pahissa,
Alexandre de Riquer, Santiago Rusiñol, Josep Triadó

Music played an integral part in the impulses underpinning Catalan
modernismo from its inception. Local songs, legends, and folklore appeared
as seemingly spontaneous expressions of popular sentiment. Synthesized
with art and literature, music helped to shape the language of its time.
Choirs and glee clubs, as well as literary, historical, and theatrical groups,
gave direction to the "voice" of the people.

The most famous of the choral societies was the Orfeo Català, founded
in Barcelona in 1891 around a nucleus of male voices, to which women,
boys, and an occasional soloist were added. It was devoted mostly to the
exploitation of old folk and religious music. Like many aspects of the
modernista movement, the real impetus came from outside, with the appearance in Barcelona of Dmitri Slaviansky's all-male Russian Chorus in
1895. Their modern performance of Russian folk music and outspoken
enthusiasm for that of Catalonia quickly caught the local imagination. The
composer Enric Morera (1865–1942) harmonized a traditional Majorcan
melody, "Sant Roman," for the Russians to perform during the visit. It
would be presented again on 22 March 1896 by the Orfeo Català, and
probably still again on 18 January 1918, when the New York Schola
Cantorum gave a concert of the Orfeo Català's repertoire in Carnegie Hall.

Morera went on to arrange or compose nearly twenty popular folksongs,
including all of the *Cançons catalans* in this exhibition. The songs share an
ethnographic heritage with those of France, the Piedmont, and Portugal,
but seem singularly lyrical and spontaneous within their discreetly propor-
tional structures. They employ ancient musical modes especially suited to
the stories they tell. Morera was involved enough in the movement to
found his own choir, Catalunya Nova, in 1896, complementing his other
modernista undertakings. These included a lyric drama based upon
Rusiñol's *L'alegria que passa* and collaboration on a Catalan opera, *La
fada*, with Massó y Torrents, presented at the fourth Festa Modernista in
Sitges in 1897.

The covers exhibited are illustrated by Alexandre de Riquer (*Sant
Ramon*, 1897, published 1911, and *Musa catalana*, 1908), Joan Llimona
(*Plany*, 1911), Santiago Rusiñol (*El rossinyol*, 1911), Lluis Bonnin (two
versions of *La mala nova*, 1898), Jaume Pahissa (*Montanyes de Canigó*,
1898), Josep Triadó (*La nostra nau*), Carles Maria Baró (*Pau Gibert*, 1908,
and *La bella pastora*, 1910), and Adrià Gual (*El tarongeret*, *El dupte de
Sant Joseph*, *Alegria de Sant Joseph*, and *La jutgesa*). Some of the drawings
were created specifically for their songs, as shown by the word play im-
plicit in Rusiñol's illustration of *El rossinyol* ("The Nightingale").

Private collection

Published between 1897 and 1911.
Printed sheet music, standard quarto
size.

As might be expected, there are many evident similarities with contemporary periodical illustration. Comparisons with the magazine *L'Avenç* are understandable, for it was published by the same firm as the music. Although *L'Avenç* was not profusely illustrated, it nevertheless carried drawings by the first five artists listed above; there were articles on contemporary composers and Catalonian folksongs, and the magazine employed the printer Ignacio Iglesias, who would be Morera's biographer in 1921. The interweaving of periodicals, their illustrators, and musical subjects was the rule rather than the exception.   E.A.

La jutgesa, illustrated by Gual

La nostra nau, illustrated by Triadó

La mala nova, illustrated by Bonnin

El rossinyol, illustrated by Rusiñol

52 Magazine: *Pèl & Ploma*

Pèl & Ploma was the successor to the periodical *Quatre Gats* and was itself in turn replaced by *Forma*. Published in Catalan (except for a brief period in 1900, when a few issues appeared in Castilian and were distributed in New York City), *Pèl & Ploma*, under the direction of its editors, Utrillo and Casas, emphasized the work of Catalan artists connected with Els Quatre Gats.

Later issues of the magazine were broader in scope and featured archaeological finds, music, and poetry. An increasing internationalism was also evident; greater numbers of European artists were featured and articles written in French were published as well. Catalan art was thus viewed in relation to European art, particularly French, as a whole.   D.H.

Private collection

1899–1903; published in Barcelona. 37.36 x 29.5 cm.

Bibliography: Merli, *Picasso: el artista y la obra de nuestro tiempo*, 10; Ráfols, *Modernismo y modernistas*, 147, 152–66; McCully, "Els Quatre Gats," 1975, 215–18; Cervera, *Modernismo*, 177–79.

PEL & PLOMA

PERIODIC MENSVAL
AM DIBVIXOS

PVBLICAT PER
RAMON CASAS &
MIQVEL VTRILLO
– 96 – PASSEIG DE
GRACIA – 96 – BAR-
CELONA

JANER

Nº 89   ANY QVART

53 Magazine: *Hispania*

Hispania, published between 1899 and 1903 in Barcelona, was one of the more conservative new periodicals, yet its issues covered a broad range of historical and contemporary Spanish art. It was one of the first journals to report on interior design and decorative arts.

Hispania, no. 73 (28 February 1902), is of particular interest, for it is devoted entirely to the work of the young Catalonian architect Josep Puig i Cadafalch (1867–1956). Raimon Casellas, a prominent art critic, wrote the main article, hailing Puig as "the most brilliant and most fertile disciple" of the archaeological school of Catalonian architects centered around Elias Rogent Amat, who designed the first neo-Romanesque building in Barcelona in 1860, and Domènech i Montaner. Photographs of interior and exterior views of buildings designed by Puig (including the Casa Martí, which housed the Quatre Gats tavern on the first floor), as well as some of his sculptural projects and preparatory sketches appear throughout the journal.

Throughout his life Puig was a fervent regionalist and historian of local Romanesque architecture. Between 1895 and 1906 he built over twelve private homes in Catalonia, wrote articles, lectured on Catalonian architecture and crafts, and participated in several political and cultural organizations. Puig viewed the current styles of northern European architects, such as Olbrich, Wagner, Horta, Van de Velde, and Baillie-Scott, as derivative of older regional architecture. He urged Catalonian architects to make use of their own heritage, in the manner of Domènech i Montaner and himself, by combining medieval forms with modern building techniques.

After 1905 Puig devoted less time to his own architecture and pursued his scholarly interests. Today he is probably known more as an art historian than an architect. He published the standard volumes on Catalonian Romanesque architecture with Antoni de Falguera and J. Goday y Casals between 1909 and 1918 (*L'arquitectura romànica a Catalunya*), and lectured at Harvard and the Sorbonne in the 1920s. Puig died in Barcelona in 1956 at the age of eighty-nine.   A.M.

Private collection

1899–1903; published in Barcelona. 32.5 x 24 cm.

Bibliography: McCully, "Els Quatre Gats," 1975, 212–13; Cervera, *Modernismo*, 183–84.

PROYECTO DE DECORACIÓN   JOSÉ PUIG Y CADAFALCH

54 Magazine: *Catalunya Artística*

Catalunya Artística was an art journal written in Catalan and published from 1900 to 1905 in Barcelona. The magazine's best feature was its reproduction of drawings and paintings by local artists. Two issues of *Catalunya Artística* (nos. 6 and 7, 18 and 25 August 1904) were dedicated to the architect Puig i Cadafalch; a short essay on Puig appears in the first, with photographs of his work scattered throughout both issues. Two years earlier *Hispania* [53] had also featured Puig's work.   A.M.

Private collection

1900–05; published in Barcelona. 27.3 x 20 cm.

Bibliography: McCully, "Els Quatre Gats," 1975, 220.

ARS

CATALUNYA ARTISTICA

J. Renart

Núm. 7 (Segona época)   **15 céntims**

55 Magazine: *Joventut*

Unlike *Pèl & Ploma*, *Joventut* was not primarily an art magazine. Its artistic policy was similar to its literary and political philosophy: to convey important developments in the North while encouraging Catalan expression. Thus, *Joventut*'s early issues, under the artistic direction of Alexandre de Riquer, featured not only drawings by Beardsley and Böcklin's *Island of the Dead* but also such local contributions as the first published drawings of Pablo Picasso. Despite annual bindings reminiscent of the British quarterly *Yellow Book*, the format and editorial style of *Joventut* most closely resembled a French example, the pre-1900 *La Plume*.   M.F.

Private collection

1900–06; published in Barcelona. 27 x 19 cm.

Bibliography: Marfany, "*Joventut*: revista modernista," 53–56; McCully, "Els Quatre Gats," 1975, 218–20; Cervera, *Modernismo*, 179–83.

JoVENTUT

Núm. 151 — Extraordinari   50 céntims

Selected Bibliography

Alcover, Joan. "Rusiñol i el modernisme a Espanya," *Obres completes*, Barcelona, 1951.

Album Nonell. Museo de Arte Moderno, Barcelona. Collection of reviews and memorabilia concerning Isidro Nonell.

Amades, Joan. *Titelles i ombres xineses*. Barcelona, 1933.

Archivo Rusiñol, 3 vols. Biblioteca Popular Santiago Rusiñol, Sitges. Collection of reviews, memorabilia, and photographs concerning Santiago Rusiñol and the history of the Cau Ferrat.

Avelí Artís, Andreu. "En Pi, titellaire dels IV Gats," *El Teatre Català*, no. 26 (24 Aug. 1912), 10–11.

———. *Retrats de Ramón Casas*. Barcelona, 1970.

Banlin-Lacroix, Catherine. "Miguel Utrillo i Morlius: critique d'art," Master's thesis, University of Paris, 1971.

Barcelona. *Breu relació dels dibuixos i estudis al oli fi que alguns pintors han exposat a la sala dels Quatre Gats*. Els Quatre Gats, 1897.

———. *Ricardo Canals*. Museo de Arte Moderno, 1976.

———. *Des dels Quatre Gats al Dau al Cet*. Col·legi d'Arquitectes, 1971.

———. *Guía del Museo de Arte Moderno*, 1945.

———. *Exposición J. Mir (1873–1940)*. Museo de Arte Moderno, 1972.

———. *Exposición Ramón Casas*. Palacio de la Virreina, 1958.

———. *Quatre Gats, Primer salón "Revista."* Sala Parés, 1954.

Bas i Gich, Joaquim. "El carrer de Mont-Sió, generador de les inquietuds artístiques barcelonines," *Meridia* (20 May 1938), 4.

———. "Mes aspectes Quatre Gats, Pere Romeu, cabaretier," *Meridia* (5 June 1938), 4.

———. "Els Quatre Gats," *D'Aci d'Alla* (19 Jan. 1931), 6ff.

Bayard, Jean-Emile. *Montmartre: Past and Present*. New York, n.d.

Benet, Rafael. *El escultor Manolo Hugué*. Barcelona, 1942.

———. *Isidro Nonell y su época*. Barcelona, 1947.

———. "Los 'Quatre Gats' y su época," *Canigó* (Oct. 1964), 1–2.

———. "La revisión de la época de 'Els Quatre Gats,'" *Goya*, no. 2 (Sept.–Oct. 1954), 96–99.

Bladé i Desumbila, Artur. *El senyor Moragas*. Barcelona, 1970.

Blunt, Anthony and Pool, Phoebe. *Picasso: The Formative Years*. London, 1962. [Cited as Blunt and Pool, *Picasso*.]

Bou i Gibert, Lluís Emili. "Les anades de Nonell a Paris," *D'Art*, no. 2 (May 1973), 3–19.

Caballé y Clos, Tomás. *Cuarenta años de Barcelona: 1890–1930*. Barcelona, 1944.

Cabañas Guevara, Luis. *Los viejos cafés de Barcelona*. Barcelona, 1946.

Casellas, Raimon. *Etapes estètiques*. Barcelona, 1916.

———. "José Puig y Cadafalch," *Hispania*, vol. 4, no. 73 (28 Feb. 1902), 76–89.

Cervera, Joseph Phillip. *Modernismo: The Catalan Renaissance of the Arts*. New York, 1976. [Cited as Cervera, *Modernismo*.]

Cerveri de Girona. "Viaje sentimental al café literario," *Revista*, no. 206 (22–28 March 1956), 12–13.

Cirici, Alexandre [Cirici-Pellicer, Alejandro]. "La arquitectura de Puig i Cadafalch," *Cuadernos de Arquitectura*, no. 63 (1st quarter 1966), 49–52.

———. *El arte modernista catalán*. Barcelona, 1951.

———. *Picasso avant Picasso*. Geneva, 1950.

———. "Picasso i Catalunya," *Serra d'Or* (10 Dec. 1966), 53.

Cirlot, Juan Eduardo. *Picasso: el nacimiento de un genio*. Barcelona, 1972.

Clarasó, Enric. *Notes viscudes*. Barcelona, 1934.

Daix, Pierre and Boudaille, Georges. *Picasso: The Blue and Rose Periods*. Neuchâtel, 1966. [Cited as Daix.]

Darío, Rubén. *España contemporánea*. Madrid, 1901.

———. *Pensadores y artistas*. Madrid, n.d.

Daudet, Léon. *L'Entre-deux-guerres*. Paris, 1915.

———. *Salons et journaux*. Paris, 1917.

Deschamps, Léon. "L'Affiche espagnole," *La Plume* (1 July 1899), 417–23.

Díaz-Plaja, Guillermo. *Modernismo frente a noventa y ocho*. Madrid, 1966.

Enseñat, Juan B. "Crónica parisiense: el Chat Noir y su escuela," *La Ilustración Artística* (1896), 470–72.

Fontbona, Francesc. *La crisi del modernisme artístic*. Barcelona, 1975.

———. "Algunes consideracions sobre el modernisme artístic," *Serra d'Or* (March 1977), 41–44.

Galwey, Enric. *El que he vist a can Parés en els darrers quaranta anys*. Barcelona, 1934.

Garcia Llansó, Antonio. *El Cau Ferrat*. Barcelona, n.d.

Garcia Niñon, Antonio. *El pintor Dario de Regoyos y su época*. Oviedo, 1958.

Garrut, José Maria. *Dos siglos de pintura catalana (XIX-XX)*. Madrid, 1974.

Gaya Nuño, Juan Antonio. *La pintura española del siglo XX*. Madrid, 1970.

Jardí, Enric. *Història del Cercle Artístic de Sant Lluc*. Barcelona, 1976.

———. *Història de Els 4 Gats*. Barcelona, 1972.

———. *Nonell*. Barcelona, 1969.

Jeanne, Paul. *Les Théâtres d'ombres à Montmartre (1887-1923)*. Paris, 1937.

Jordà, Josep Maria. "Ramón Casas," *Butlletí dels museus d'art de Barcelona*, no. 11 (April 1932), 105-10.

———. *Ramón Casas, pintor*. Barcelona, 1931.

———. "Ricard Canals," *Butlletí dels museus d'art de Barcelona*, no. 23 (April 1933), 102-11.

Junoy, José Maria. *Arte y artistas*. Barcelona, 1912.

Lafuente Ferrari, Enrique. "Para una revisión de Picasso," *Revista de Occidente*, no. 135-36 (June-July 1974), 241-345.

Larco, Jorge. *La pintura española moderna y contemporánea*, 3 vols. Madrid, 1964.

Litvak, Lily. *A Dream of Arcadia*. Austin, 1975.

Lladó, José Maria. "El Picasso de Els Quatre Gats," *Tele-Express* (23 Oct. 1971).

Madrid. *El modernismo en España*. Casón del Buen Retiro, 1969.

Maragall, Joan A. *Història de la Sala Parés*. Barcelona, 1975.

———. "La Sala Parés en la vida artística de Barcelona," speech given at the Sala Parés on 19 Feb. 1967.

Maragall, Joan. "La obra de Santiago Rusiñol," *Diario de Barcelona* (19 April 1900).

Marfany, Joan Lluis. *Aspectes del modernisme*. Barcelona, 1975.

———. "*Joventut*: revista modernista," *Serra d'Or* (15 Dec. 1970), 53-56.

———. "A proposit d'un llibre de Francesc Fontbona," *Serra d'Or* (Dec. 1976), 71-74.

———. "Sobre el significat del terme 'modernisme,'" *Reçerques*, no. 2 (1972), 73-91.

Masriera y Manovens, José. *Arte moderno*. Barcelona, 1902.

Masriera y Rosés, Luis. *La caida del modernismo*. Barcelona, 1913.

McCully, Marilyn. "El poster y Els Quatre Gats," *Destino* (21 June 1969), 70-73.

———. "Els Quatre Gats," manuscript awarded the Alfons Bonay i Carbó prize, Institut d'Estudis Catalans, Barcelona, 1969.

———. "Els Quatre Gats and Modernista Painting in Catalonia in the 1890s," Ph.D. dissertation, Yale University, 1975.

Merli, Joan. *Picasso: el artista y la obra de nuestro tiempo*. Buenos Aires, 1942.

Moragas, Rafael. "Miquel Utrillo, l'animador," *Meridia* (1 July 1935), 3.

Nonell, Carolina. *Isidro Nonell: su vida y su obra*. Madrid, 1963.

Opisso, Alfredo. *Arte y artistas catalanes*. Barcelona, 1900.

Opisso, Ricardo. "Tardes de los 'Quatre Gats,'" *Diario de Barcelona* (24 Feb. 1952), 38.

Palau Fabre, Josep. "1900: A Friend of His Youth," *Homage to Picasso*. Special issue of *XXᵉ Siècle Review*. New York, 1971, 3-12.

———. *Picasso en Cataluña*. Barcelona, 1966.

———. *Picasso i els seus amics catalans*. Barcelona, 1971.

———. *Picasso per Picasso*. Barcelona, 1970.

Penrose, Roland. *Picasso: His Life and Work*. New York, 1973.

Pla, Josep. *Santiago Rusiñol*. Barcelona, 1961.

———. *Santiago Rusiñol y su tiempo*. Barcelona, 1942.

———. *Santiago Rusiñol y el seu temps*. Barcelona, 1955.

———. *Vida de Manolo*. Barcelona, 1930.

Planes, Ramón [Planas]. *El modernisme a Sitges*. Barcelona, 1969.

———. *Santiago Rusiñol per ell mateix*. Barcelona, 1971.

Puig i Cadafalch, Josep. *L'Oeuvre de Puig Cadafalch: architecte 1896-1904*. Barcelona, 1904.

Pujols, Francisco. "Francisco Pujols evoca las figuras literarias de hace veinticinco años," *La Noche* (26 Oct. 1927).

Pylax. "New Posters," *The Poster Collector's Circular*, no. 2 (Feb. 1899), 23-27.

Ráfols, José F. *El arte modernista en Barcelona*. Barcelona, 1943.

———. "Los carteles '1900,'" *Destino* (31 Dec. 1955), 35-36.

———. "Degas y Rusiñol," *Anales y boletín de los museos de arte de Barcelona*, no. 3-4 (July-Dec. 1948), 503-4.

———. *Diccionario biográfico de artistas de Cataluña*, 3 vols. Barcelona, 1951-53.

———. *Modernismo y modernistas*. Barcelona, 1949.

————. "Petits dibuixos de Ramón Casas a la col·lecció del museu de Barcelona," *Butlletí dels museus d'art de Barcelona*, no. 12 (May 1932), 139–46.

————. "Puig y Cadafalch," *Cuadernos de arquitectura* (4th quarter 1956), 1–7.

————. "Ramón Casas," *Goya*, no. 18 (May–June 1957), 344–51.

————. *Ramón Casas, dibujante*. Barcelona, n.d.

————. *Ramón Casas, pintor*. Barcelona, n.d.

Rierola, Francesc. *Dietari*. Barcelona, 1955.

Roda, Pedro de. "El modernismo y los llamados modernistas en la Barcelona de 'fin de siglo,'" *La Noche* (23 Nov. 1927).

Rubin, William. "Shadows, Pantomimes and the Art of 'Fin de siècle,'" *Magazine of Art*, no. 3 (March 1953), 114–22.

Rusiñol, Maria. *Santiago Rusiñol vist per la seva filla*. Barcelona, 1950.

Rusiñol, Santiago. *Obres completes*. Barcelona, 1956.

Sabartés, Jaime. *Picasso: documents iconographiques*. Geneva, 1954.

————. *Picasso: portraits et souvenirs*. Paris, 1946.

Salas, Xavier de. "Some Notes on a Letter," *Burlington Magazine*, no. 102 (Nov. 1960), 482–84.

Saltiró, Juan. "*Quatre Gats*" o una tertulia de alegres bohemios. Barcelona, 1945.

Santos Torroella, Rafael. *El cartel*. Barcelona, 1949.

————. "Picasso y Barcelona," *El Noticiero Universal* (18 March 1970), 21.

Sempronio. "Tertulias y peñas entre dos siglos," *Destino* (21 June 1963), 67–69.

Shattuck, Roger. *The Banquet Years*. New York, 1968.

Sitges. *Catálogo de pintura y dibujo del "Cau Ferrat,"* 1942.

————. *Guía sumària del Cau Ferrat*, 1933.

Storm, John. *The Valadon Drama*. New York, 1958.

Templier, Pierre D. *Erik Satie*, trans. by E. L. French and D. S. French. Cambridge, Mass., 1969.

Thirlmere, Rowland. *Letters from Catalonia*. London, 1905.

Torent, Joan. "Un número de *L'Esquella de la Torratxa* dedicado al modernismo," *Destino* (23 Oct. 1969), 46.

Utrillo Morlius, Miguel. "Història anecdòtica del Cau Ferrat," *Museo de Arte Moderno*, Barcelona, 1934.

————. "L'obra d'en Casas," *Forma*, vol. 1 (1904), 310–25.

Utrillo y Vidal, Miguel. "El pintor Ramón Casas a través de mis recuerdos y su epistolario," *Anales y boletín de los museos de arte de Barcelona*, no. 1 (Jan. 1944), 15–27.

————. "Las 'sombras chinescas' vistas por dentro," *La Vanguardia* (24 April 1971), 4; (28 April 1971), 4.

Valentí Fiol, Eduard. *El primer modernismo literario catalán y sus fundamentos ideológicos*. Barcelona, 1973.

Verdaguer, Mario. *Medio siglo de vida íntima barcelonesa*. Barcelona, 1957.

Zervos, Christian. *Pablo Picasso*. 31 vols. to date. Paris, 1932– . [Cited as Z.]

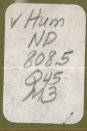

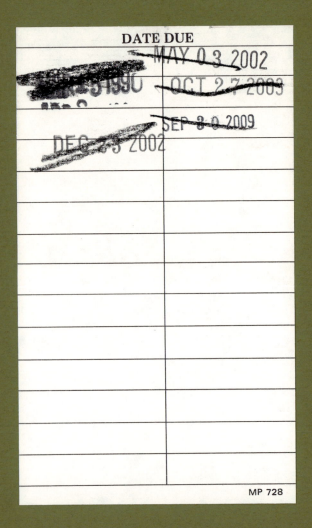